CARTOONS.

BY

MARGARET J. PRESTON.

BOSTON:
ROBERTS BROTHERS.
1875.

Cambridge:
Press of John Wilson & Son.

TO

ELIZABETH RANDOLPH PRESTON ALLAN.

CONTENTS.

Cartoons from the Life of the Legends.

Cartoons from the Life of To-Day.

Cartoons from the Life of To-Day (continued).

THE GOOD OF IT.

WHEN any task my hands essay,
Wherewith to fill the eager day,
There rises to my thought alway,

This hindering question:—Whence the need
Of this thy lightly-weighted deed?
Forego it, and who taketh heed?

Perform it,—who will praise or blame,
Though it be wrought with purest aim?
Done or undone, 'tis all the same!

It cannot surely much behoove,
If, in thy life's so shallow groove,
Thou movest, or thou dost not move.

Amidst the thousand myriad lives
That overcrowd earth's human hives,
What matter if no work survives

Of thy small doing? — Who counts, alas,
One cricket chirping in the grass,
The less, when summer-time doth pass?

So, keep thy song unwritten; spare
To spill thy music on the air;
Let go the stainless canvas bare.

The world is over-deaved with speech;
And who so out of wisdom's reach,
As yet to lack what *thou* canst teach?

O poor, proud reasoning! Shall the spray
Of fern beside the boulder gray,
Thrid with the morning's opals, say, —

"Whole wingèd flocks their nests have made
In yon great oak. Why should *my* blade
Afford an humble-bee its shade?"

Or the light breeze sigh: "Loud and deep,
The mountain-winds the forests sweep;
Must *I* just rock one rose asleep?"

Or glow-worm murmur: "So divine,
So flooding, sunlight's, moonlight's shine,—
This moth can need no glint of *mine!*"

Because our music is not keyed
Beethoven-wise, therefore, indeed,
We scorn to blow the oaten reed.

Because we may not counterpart
The dance and trance of Shakespeare's art,
We will not soothe one aching heart!

—Mock meekness all! There doth not live
Any so poor but they may give,
Any so rich but may receive.

Withhold the very meagrest dole
Hands can bestow, in part or whole,
And we may stint a starving soul.

What then? — If one weak song of mine
Should yet prevail to bring the shine
Back o'er some spirit's dull decline,

And for a moment seem to fling
A flash about its sun-setting, —
I think (God granting) I may sing.

FROM THE LIFE

OF THE

OLD MASTERS.

MONA LISA'S PICTURE.

FRANCESCO.

GOOD Messer Leonardo, — dawdling still
Over that canvas? Pray how many times
Have the black olives dropped in yonder garden
Since you began it?

LEONARDO.[1]

Do I gauge my work
By olive-harvests? If you reckon toil
By its results, then count me out its sum,
Beseech you. On the very day I planned
The altar-piece for Nunziata's Church,
You came with Mona Lisa first. But since, —
Why, there's Valdarno bridge, and the great mill
Nigh to Fucecchio, and the wide canal,
That floated off my thoughts, as they had been
Merceries for the market. Then that plague
Anent Duke Sforza's bronze; and the designs
The Flanders merchants harried me about;
Besides, my *Di Natura*, and — what else?

FRANCESCO.

"Besides," forsooth! Why, there are twenty more
Unfinished schemes. If thus you mean to count,
I'd say the portrait of my wife had been
In your *bottèga*, — well, — some dozen years;
And yet, I do believe, 'tis barely four.
But, look you! all this time the panel waits:
'Tis done, — now grant it so; the picture's done.

LEONARDO.

Done? — Nothing that my pencil ever touches
Is wholly done. There's some evasive grace
Always beyond, which still I fail to reach,
As heretofore, I've failed to hold and fix
Your Mona Lisa's changeful loveliness.
Why, think of it, my lord. Here's Nature's self
Has patient wrought these two-and-twenty years,
With subtlest transmutations, making her
Your pride, the pride of Florence and — my despair!
Her native sky, Salerno's azurn sky,
Gave (to begin) that half-Greek dower of hers;
And every atmosphere that she has breathed
Since, — all the potent essences that light,
Air, color, perfume, set of mellowing suns,

Crisp morns, rich noons, and fruited evening-times, —
All agencies that happiness and love
Commingled bring, — all mystic confluence
Of passionate life with her imperial calm,
All interfuse of high intelligence,
All entertainments of divinest thought,
That cause Saint Catherine's ecstasies seem pale, —
Why these, I say, have been so many masters,
Each perfect in his art, who, on the curves
Of her pure face, with silent chiselling,
Have toiled these two-and-twenty years! while I,
Nature's unskilled disciple —

FRANCESCO.

Hold! Draw breath!
"*Unskilled?*" Nay, man, you dig too many channels,
Dividing so your overmastering powers
To your own discontent; — that's all. I would
This restive genius had been parcelled out
Midst a half dozen grateful citizens,
To make their fortunes wherewithal; and then
Less time would serve my lady's face.

LEONARDO.

My lord,
"*If what thou wouldst, thou canst not, be content*

To strive for what thou canst." So sang I once.*
I strive for what I can. But you, — you tire,
You gibe, because through a brief season's space —

(FRANCESCO.

Four mortal years since he began the picture!)

LEONARDO.

I've not attained unto the capture yet
Of that shy, furtive beauty. Oft you've watched
The miracle of her smile? Now, see you here,
'Tis only just half caught, — *not* half, observe:
Next time that Mona Lisa sits, I'll work
Into it finer grace; I'll trap the charm
Somehow. You'll see —

FRANCESCO.

Good faith! but don't you hear
The panel waits? I'm tired of seeing the arras
Hang blankly over it. San Luca's feast
Falls four days hence, and on its eve I hold
A banquet. Mark, — the portrait must be placed
Ere then —

* "Chi non può quel che vuol, quel che può voglia." — *From a Sonnet by Leonardo.*

LEONARDO.

Ay, have it, — have it, an you will,
In season for your guests, betwixt their cups,
To sum its lack. I marvel you should fail
To note its incompleteness! Why, this flesh
Would pulsate else; this lash betray a droop
Under full gaze, — these pearls would ebb and flow
With every rippling lapse of tided breath,
Astrand on the white beaching of her throat!
— But have the panel filled (if that's the point),
And barter, for one night's fresh novelty,
An immortality of loveliness
For Mona Lisa; since, once carried hence,
My brush shall never touch the canvas more.

THE MAESTRO'S CONFESSION.

(ANDREA DAL CASTAGNO. 1460.)

I.

THREE-SCORE and ten, —
I wish it were all to live again!
Doesn't the Scripture somewhere say,
By reason of strength that mortals may
  Even reach fourscore? Alack! who knows!
Ten sweet, long years of life! I would paint
My Lady and many and many a saint,
  And thereby win my soul's repose.
Yet, Fra Bernardo, you shake your head;
    Has the leech once said
    I must die? But he
Is only a fallible man, you see.
  Now, if it had been our Father, the Pope,
  I should *know* there was then no hope.
Were only I sure of a few kind years
More to be merry in, then my fears —

Faugh! — wouldn't I slip them all awhile
For mocking me so, — and turn and smile
At their hated reckonings? Whence the need
Of squaring accounts for word and deed,
Till the lease is up? — What? — *Now?* . . . You fright
Me strangely! I couldn't have heard aright, —
"*To-night?*" No, no! — Did you say, — "*To-night?*"

II.

Ah, woe! ah, well!
"*Confess — confess, and so be forgiven:*"
Is there no easier path to heaven?
Santa Maria! — how can I tell
What now for a score
Of years and more,
I've buried away in my heart so deep,
That howso weary I've been, I've kept
Eyes waking, when near me another slept,
Lest I might mutter it in my sleep?
And now at the last, to blab it clear!
How the women will shirk my pictures! And worse
Will the men do, — spit on my name and curse:
But then, — up in heaven I shall not hear!
— I faint — I faint —
Quick, Fra Bernardo! — the figure stands

There in the niche, — my patron saint:
Put it within my trembling hands
Till they are steadier, — so . . .
My brain
Dizzied and whirled with sudden pain,
Trying to span that gulf of years, —
Fronting once more those long-laid fears.
Confess, — why, yes, — if I must, I *must;*
Now good San Christopher be my trust!
But fill me first, from yon crystal cup,
Strong wine to bolster my courage up.
— (That thing is a gem of craftsmanship;
Just note how its curvings fit the lip!)

Ah! you, in your sodden, stagnant life,
What should *you* know of the rage and strife,
The blinding envy, the lashing smart
That swirls and sweeps through the Maestro's heart,
When he sees his housemate snatch the prize
Out from under his very eyes,
For which he would wreck his soul? You see,
I taught him his art from first to last:
Whatever he was, he owed to me;
And then to be browbeat, — overpassed, —

Stealthily jeered behind the hand!
Why, that was more than a saint could stand,
And I was no saint. And if my soul,
With a pride like the devil's, spurned control,
And goaded me on to madness, till
I lost all measure of good or ill, —
Whose fault was it, pray? O, many a day
I've cursed it, yet whose is the blame, I say?

His name? — How odd that you question so!
When I'm sure I have spoken it over and o'er,
And why should you care to hear it more?

III.

Well, — as I was saying, — Domenico
  Was wont of my skill to make such light,
  That seeing him go, on a certain night,
Out with his lute, I followed. Hot
From a battle of words, I heeded not
  Whither I went, till I heard him twang
A madrigal under the lattice, where
  Only the night before *I* sang.
— A double robbery! and I swear
'Twas overmuch for the flesh to bear.

Why ask me? I knew not what I did;
But I hastened home with my rapier hid
  Under my cloak, — and the blade was wet:
. . . Just open that cabinet there, and see
  The strange, red rustiness on it yet.

A calm that was dead as dead could be,
Numbed me. I seized my chalks to trace
— What think you? — *Judas Iscariot's face!*
I just had gotten the scowl, no more,
When the shuffle of feet drew near my door, —
  (We long had been messmates, as I've said,)
Then, — wide they flung it, and on the floor
  Laid down Domenico, — dead!

Back reeled my senses; a scorching pain
Tingled like lightning through my brain;
And ere the spasm of fear was broke,
The men who had borne him homeward, spoke
Soothingly: — "Some assassin's knife
Had taken the innocent artist's life,
— Wherefore, 'twere hard to say; — all men
Had troubles to vex them now and then,
Unguessed of the world. Unto his friend,

The bitterest sufferer (since *he* knew
Only how faithful he was, and true),
Neighbors stood ready to extend
Pity and comfort." . . .
Then came my tears, —
And I've been sorry these twenty years!

Now, Fra Bernardo, you have my sin:
— Do you think Saint Peter will let me in?

VITTORIA COLONNA TO MICHAEL ANGELO.

(ROME. 1546.)

ALL past and gone for us, — all past and gone!
The shadow on the dial doth not move
Back, while I cloud the sunny Heretofore
With the Hereafter. Yet I am content
To watch the shadow broaden into the dark,
Secure of the fair morrow overhead.
Best friend! — be thou so, also: For we twain,
Who, through the foulness of this festering age,
Drew each the other with such instinct true
As kept from utter wreck faith in our kind, —
We twain, — one lingering on the violet verge,
And one with eyes raised to the twilight peaks, —
Shall meet i' the morn again. 'Tis the old tune
Wherewith sweet Mother Nature soothes to sleep
Her tired-out children.

Yet, at memory's touch

The dial *doth* seem to move; and o'er again
I live our evenings in the sacristy
Of San Silvestro, where, in high discourse,
Shallowed beyond the creeping ebb of time,
We reasoned oft, of such exalted themes
As caught us hence: and if 'twere in the body
Or out of it we spake, we scarce could tell.

The hum of voices on the Esquiline Way, —
The sunbeam's finger pointing hushingly
Along the frescoed wall, — the fitful plash
Of the choked fountain gurgling through the weeds, —
The horses pawing at some palace-gate —
Such outward things, thou well rememberest how,
In breaches of our talk, they made us know
Who, — what we were. Not spirits divest of clay:
But thou, Art's last apostle, chosen of God
To write a new Apocalypse for man,
In thy self-exile, banished from thy kind,
My lonely Angelo! — and I, a woman,
Widowed and waxen sick of earthly shows,
(Save dreams of my enchanted Ischïa),
Yet charged of Heaven with still one errand more,
Despite the hands that dropped so worn.

— Methinks,
Amid these blind, uncomprehending times,
We are the only two that, face to face,
Do know each other, as God doth know us both.
— O fearless friendship, that held nothing back!
O absolute trust, that yielded every key,
And flung each curtain up, and drew me on
To enter the white temple of thy soul,
So vast, so cold, so waste! — and give thee sense
Of living warmth, of throbbing tenderness,
Of soft dependencies! O faith that made
Thee free to seek the spot where my dead hopes
Have sepulture, and read above the crypt
Deep graven, the tearful legend of my life!
There, gloomed with the memorials of my past,
Thou once for all didst learn what man accepts
Lothly (— how should *he* else?) — that never woman,
Fashioned a woman, — heart, brain, body, soul, —
Ever twice loved. False gods there be enow:
But o'er the altar of her worship, see,
Highest and chiefest of her decalogue,
That First Commandment written: — "*No love but one!*"

Nor hath a treacherous *if* ensnared our path:[2]
My broken life gave up, thou knew'st its best:

Little, I trow; but thy so grand content
Greatened the gift. Supremest truth I gave;
Reverence, whose crystal sheen was never blurred
By faintest film of over-breathing doubt;
Quick comprehension of thine unsaid thought,
That seemed a half omniscience; helpfulness
Such as thou hadst not known, of womanly hands;
And sympathies so urgent, they made bold
To press their way where never mortal yet
Entrance had gained, — even to thy soul. Ah, sad
And hunger-bitten soul! whose lion pride
Scorned, from its lair, the world-folk cowering by!
— If I, grown brave through discipline of grief,
Fearless, did lure thee forth, and make thee feel
Some poor sufficing of thy human needs, —
Christ's grace have thanks therefor; — no meed of mine.

— "*Vittoria scultorè:* * — thus thou writ'st;
Even that thy life bears witness to my hand,
Chisel and file. Ah, friend! — if unawares,
Some little trick of Art I've caught from thee,

* "Tal di stesso nacqui e venni prima
Umil model, per opra più perfetta
Rinoscer poi di voi, donna alta e degna."

Michael Angelo to Vittoria.

Sweet theft it was, as honest work confessed,
That lets me know why grief forbore to slay.
I understood not, when the angel stooped,
Whispering, — "Live on! for yet one joyless soul,
Void of true faith in human happiness,
Waits to be won by thee, from unbelief."

Now, all is clear. For *thy* sake I am glad
I waited. Not that some far age may say, —
"*God's benison on her, since she was the friend
Of Michael Angelo!*" But better far,
And holier so, that like Beatricè,
(How oft I've heard thee read the blessèd vision!)
'Twas mine to point thee to that Paradise
Whither I go, — whither thou'lt follow soon.

SEBASTIANO AT SUPPER.[8]

I.

— Ha! ha! — how free and happy I am,
Here in my roystering, rollic calm,
With never a scowling monk to gibe,
Or harry me for the crab-like way
They tell me I work. That beggarly tribe,
Priors and abbesses, deem that a day
Must count in the life of a picture: Fools!
Do they think that they grow like mushroom stools?
— "*Here's so many feet of blank, bare wall,* —
Here's so many days to fresco all."
Bah! Through the Father's grace *that's* past,
And I'm free, — do you hear, friends? — free at last,
With only the *Seals* upon my mind;
As idle a Fratè as you'll find
In Rome or out of it. Here are we,
Gandolfo and Messer Luigi, — three
Right merry old comrades, faith, we be:
The night is before us: with shout and chorus,
We'll set the rafters a-ringing o'er us:

For I vow I never could tell which art,—
The brush or the bow, most swayed my heart.
—Yes—Yes,—His Worship, Ippolito,
Once served me a sorry trick, I trow,
The time he sent—(he was love a-craze,
And wanted the work quick done)—relays
Of horses for speed, when he made me paint
The Donna Guëlma: *she* was the saint
His prayers were prayed to, in those old days!
—Well,—would you believe it?—nathless, 'tis true;
I left my pigments behind, and brought
My viol, as uppermost in my thought:
—And what did his Cardinal Eminence do?
He smashed and he crashed the strings right through!
And so, thereafter, I could not shirk,
For sake of my music, a day of work:
Ay, ay,—be sure, 'twas a brutal shame!
But it helped, in a month, to build my fame;
For I need not tell you the picture's name.

II.

Heigho!—with what a relief I sigh,
As I lounge so masterless here,—you by,
Dearest of gossips,—sigh to think

How Michelagnolo pinned me down,
Granting me scarcely leave to wink,
Impaled all day on his frescoes brown, —
Lout that I was to fear his frown!
No toil can tire *him* out: he'll be
Still fresh — you mark me — at ninety-three,
With muscles like his own *David's*. Well
It was that we quarrelled: for who can tell,
If, under his all-compelling will,
I might not be mixing his mortars still?
His love for me, sooth, was small enow:
For I made him my debtor long ago,
And it rankles his crabbed pride. You see,
I voyaged to Ischïa once, to paint
The lovely Marchèsa: (What a saint
Of a wife Pescara had! And he . . .
But we'll tell no tales: It's all forgiven,
Now that he's been these years in heaven!)
The picture I gave to Michael, who
Had learned to worship that face, as you
Worship Our Lady's; nor would I touch
In boot, a *baioccho:* 'tis so much
To have him beholden! And that is how
The liking of old he grudges now.

III.

Ah, well! It is past; and I've loved my Art;
 Beautiful mistress she ever was;
And yet we are not unloth to part,
 Though bound together for years: because
I inwardly groan to come and go
At beck of the best; and I leave her, so.
Besides, — I own, of the perilous stuff
The world calls fame, I have had enough:
To Franco, Perino, and such, 'tis best,
I think, on the whole, to leave the rest!

— I'm garrulous. Why have you let me waste
My breath a-chattering? Only taste
This vintage (— I swear it might cheat the Fates!)
And, see you, my friends, — the supper waits.

IN THE SISTINE.

(Raffaelle and Giulio Romano.)

Raffaelle.

— It is divine! — I scarce can gaze around
With knees unbent. My calm Philosophers *
Are earthliest mortals, verily, beside
These gods of Michael's. Would we twain might meet
Here, while I did him reverence, owning how
He, of all men, did first unseal my eyes
To the sublime significance of Form,
That day in Florence, when burst his *Pietà*
Like a new sense upon me.

Giulio.

Better so:
That rapier tongue of his might have its thrust,
Touching your labors in the Vatican:[4]
And though its point would blunt itself against
The proof-mail of *your* temper, it might gash

* *The School of Athens*, just completed.

Great dints in mine. He was supreme in Rome
Before you came; but now the loggie-loungers
Take sides and wrangle; and he loathes to see
His realm beset by rivals, least of all
By one whose whole decade of scanter years
Would seem —

RAFFAELLE.

Forbear, my Giulio, — 'tis not so!
Standing in such majestic Presences,
Whose models even, his genius hath evoked,
(For where can Rome or Florence show to-day,
Titans like these?) it were not possible
That I could link one thought of paltriness
With this most royal soul. Who thus creates,
Hath something kindred with the Hand Divine.
Such eyried pride stoops not to foul its beak
With envy's garbage. Doth Vesuvius grudge
The pretty vineyard at his foot, its grapes?
— For me, — I sink o'ertasked, — a-strain to gauge
The reach beyond my grasping, hinted here,
By these grand Prophet brows. See yonder sweep
Of daring touch, — how arrogant of power,
Through sense of mastery! Verily, I do think

He would not halt, afeared, nor blench, if bidden
To picture God-the-Father, face to face!

GIULIO.

That would he not! Hath he not browbeat oft
His Holiness even? Could Satan's self do more?
— O ho! Our Angelo's angelical
After Apollyon's fashion —

RAFFAELLE.

Peace! — It hurts
That you should wrong him so! Think how remote
His isolate world from ours. Companionless,
Renouncing even his self-humanity, —
He dwells apart on Art's Olympian top,
In brotherhood with gods, curtained about
With tragic mists that blot our common ways
Out from his knowledge: And when he descends,
'Tis as the gossips chatter of his work
On this grand ceiling — how through lengthened gaze
Upward, the power of earthward glance was lost:
And therefore (blame him not), he overlooks
Us lesser mortals who but haunt the slope —

GIULIO.

"*Lesser*," i' faith! Good Master, I lose patience!

Raffaelle.

Content you, we'll say *happier* then: We, rich
In miracle of sunset and of dawn, —
In wonderments of blue, ethereal air, —
In yellowing corn-fields, and sheep-dotted dells,
And interspaces flaked with flooding light,
And all the maddening sweetnesses his eyes,
— Poor, blinded eyes! — had never vision for!
We, over-rich through maidens' solacings,
And childhood's mirth, and wonted fellowships,
And the keen joyance of this summer-land:
O happier thus a thousand-fold than he,
He, midst his chilling clouds upraised too high
For human needs, — too high to be aught else
Than numbed and frost-pinched, and so doomed to miss
The fervid meltings of a foolish love
Trickling about his heart! I, overblest
Through its sufficingness, — I, garmented
So silkenly in Art's delightsomeness,
So warmed by the felicities of life,
I needs must nurse a grievous ache to think
On Michael's cold, white, statued loneliness.

GIULIO.

Dear, gentle Master, he would scout such pity:
What is all life to him, — its men, its women,
The tumult and the process of its loves,
Its hates, its strifes, — what but a quarry, whence
To hew and shape his wrestling thoughts —

RAFFAELLE.

But then,
Confess his Atlases can heave a world !

GIULIO.

Ay, grant you, giants all : Just see their brows
So wrinkle-gasht, — their knotted muscles, — thews
Like cordage stretcht. Who ever dreams to find
A nesting here for dove-eyed charities ?
Look you aloft: he holds mere Beauty, weak.
Where is the breathing flesh, the humid light,
The tremulous tints, the centred calm, which make
Whatso *my* Master touches, all divine ?
His women — see them ! Stout Minervas, who
Would flout the clinging of a baby's arms —

RAFFAELLE.

Consider, Giulio, — they do say of him
He never kissed a woman, — never caught

Some kindling warmth from foldings of her hands,
Nor from her lap hath tossed a crooning child,
With the white milk-drop on its mouth, — and then
Be merciful!

GIULIO.

And let him teach disdain
Of life's soft graciousness? Why, he would make
Us infidels to love and all sweet passions!
Save that kind Heaven has set our Raffaelle here,
A crowning antidote, to prove that not
Colossal Force nor Form can rule the realm
Of Art or Nature with such sovran power
As a fair woman's face. And so the smile
You've left on Mary-Mother's lips, though toucht
With trouble of tears, will keep within men's souls
The purer worship; — so the shine above
Your Holy Child will seem a miracle
Wherewith to seal the world's true faith for ever!

THE DUKE'S COMMISSION.

A Florentine Duke, (the tale you know,)
Bade summon in haste his sculptor: — "Lo,
Your marble! Now carve me a bust in snow."

('Twas a rare amaze for a Tuscan eye
To see heaped swathes in the archways lie,
And swirl on the balconies full knee-high.)

And the sculptor moulded it, marvellous, white,
From dark to dawn of a winter night;
And the city all gathered to see the sight.

He thought to jeer him, — the braggart Duke;
But grand was the Master's dumb rebuke:
It mattered not what *his* genius took

To body his art, — the snow from the sky,
A block from Carrara's quarries nigh;
— The work that has soul in it cannot die!

Has the Greek's strange witchery perished? Where
Is the canvas that Zeuxis wrought? Declare,
Was the voice of the Academe *only* air?

— As it's truth I tell, that statue set
In the common ways where the people met,
Has never, through ages, crumbled yet!

The hand that shaped it has turned to clay,
The ducal splendor has passed away;
But stand on the storied spot to-day,

In the square of the palace, and close your eyes,
And clear on the blue of the Tuscan skies,
You'll see the figure before you rise,

As perfect as when in its Sphinx-like grace,
It flashed for a single morning's space
On each wondering Florentine's upturned face.

('Tis only the outward perisheth:
Where genius has breathed its vital breath,
There never can come decay or death.)

And so, as it were, to soothe the taunt,
Right noble avenging time doth grant:
— The snow is enduring as adamant!

And the scoffing Duke? . . . Go search and see
If nave, basilica, sacristy,
Keep marble memory of such as he.

Has his name been graven on frieze or wall?
What echo comes back, when Fame doth call?
— The tale of the mockery, — that is all![5]

DONNA MARGHERITA.

—Here is the chamber: Messers, enter ye:
A Borgherini needs must courtesy show
To whoso comes.[6]
. . . Ye see upon the walls,
My pricelesss pictures, famed o'er Tuscany,
Jacopo's work. Behold the Patriarch's sons,
Cruel, unpitying, grouped about the boy,
Whom, for a fardel of rough, Midian gold,
They barter, mindless of his frantic prayers.

Ha, Palla!—stand where thou canst note the chaffer;
Ay,—so! . . . And now, I say, this Simeon,
Who clutches from the Arab's sleeve the price
They higgle o'er,—is as a puling milk-sop
To that *thou* art! He cheapened only blood;
Thou,—honor, faith, and . . . Florence! And because
She lies, our Florence, weeping at the feet
Of her invaders, in her broideries wrapped,

(An Empress still, wanting, albeit, a crust, —)
Thy thief's hand twitches off thy mother's robe,
Leaving her in her nuded majesty
To perish: Out upon thy villany!

I would this jewelled bodkin were a lance,
For other impalement than a woman's hair!
But, being a woman, shorn of all defence,
Saving my shuddering hate, I dare defy
Thee and thy myrmidons, though ye be armed
With the *Signòri's* huckstering warrant: Nay!
Ye wrest no pictures from these walls, except
Ye wrest, as well, my life!
. . . Palla, behold
Within that carven niche, my bridal couch:
And when I use, from my Francesco's face
To turn, I ever met the love-born glance
On Jacob's brow, — (look!) as, with thirsting lips,
He quaffs the Syrian maiden's loveliness.
The earliest sight that held the baby eyes
Of my young Tuscans, was yon Hebrew lad,
Clasping his brothers' knees. Why, I should lack
Such common mother-instincts even, as teach
The leaguered lioness to shield her lair,

If less I dare for these! My scorn's white heats
Shall shrivel your purpose, till ye shun to see
Each gazing on each,—how dastards haste to crawl
Out of its blaze.
. . . Yet Palla hath loved Art,
And he hath painted oft Our Lady's face
Divinely, as if through auroral clouds
Herself had stooped to grant him seraph-glimpse
Else unconceived—
Palla,—some wine? Meseems
There's sudden faintness: *No?* Then sit apart
Under the arch here, where thou best canst mark
Reuben, the coward, who slinks away, afeared
To brave the wrath of Judah and the rest.

. . . What!—tire ye of the masterpiece so soon
That ye turn backs on't? Ay, 'tis well ye put
Your tools up; they'll set free no frames to-day,
From Casa Borgherini's walls, I pledge:
And to the brave *Signòri*—(strong as brave!)
Bear a weak, helpless woman's duty back,
And say, she chaffers overmuch about
The Iscariot price, seeing she holds too dear
Her pictures,—even at cost of her heart's blood.

POUSSIN AND HIS MASTER.[7]

I.

— ALWAYS the way! — Just when the light is fairest —
  Just when it floods the canvas to my mind,
Starting to sudden life those charms, the rarest
  That lurk, lost, in the clare-obscure behind, —
Eluding thus the gaze of the beholder,
Some curious eye comes peering o'er my shoulder.

II.

Only a copyist: That is what they're saying;
  For looks speak loudest oft, when lips are dumb:
Small care to me the leer their scorn betraying,
  If yet the secret of *his* skill should come
Even at the last. I'd rise above disaster,
Envy, and wrong, as did the dear old master.

III.

What marvel if he lives yet! — I would wander
  Over all Italy to find his home,
And bless him for the hallowed vision yonder:
  How Raffaelle would have loved this *Saint Jerome*,

And given it praise! Yet the base herd will gather
A-gape before some flaunting Venus rather.

IV.

—One more to vex me! Tottering on his crutches,
Here comes a drivelling wretch to carp and stare;
Ha!—have a care, old man!—your staff—it touches
The outmost corner of the canvas there:
—Good lack! it sets a-flutter all my passion
To see its grandeur treated in such fashion!

V.

"*Who painted it?*" Now get you gone, and winnow
The chaff that chokes your memory! Can it be,
That, where he won his bays, Domenichino
Is so forgotten they question,—"Who is *he?*"
O heart o' mine!—what folly even to cherish
Thy lightest dream, when *such* a name can perish!

VI.

—What?—How?—Say it once more!—You—*you* the master,
—Domenichino? . . . You? Alive? . . . in Rome?
(One moment let me lean on this pilaster,
So fast my breath comes!) *Sick—without a home?*

Of honor cheated — filched of honest wages,
And this — and this *your* gift to all the ages?

VII.

Thank God that I have found you! On the border
  Of your poor garment would I leave a kiss!
Let me but serve you, — let me be your warder,
  Till you, with Raffaelle, share (your right it is!)
An homage that the centuries shall not sunder,
Till on *your* work, as his, men gaze and wonder.

VIII.

How say you? Palter, truckle to the fancies
  Of these degenerate times and — prosper so?
Nay! Give me sevenfold rather your mischances,
  So I to Art be true, — so I but know
One such creation mine, and one before it
To stand, as I, a worshipper, and adore it!

THE BARON'S DAUGHTER.

(St. Sebald's. Nuremberg.)

Albrecht Dürer.

— She promised to meet me here, when through
  The panes of yon mullion'd window came
  The sun's last flaunt in a ruby flame,
And now — it has slidden up to the blue
Of St. Michael's robe: But hist! — the feet
I hear may be hers: — Ah, Laggard, — Sweet —

Augusta.

Thou didst not doubt of me, Albrecht?

Albrecht.

Nay,

But Love is no Joshua: though he may
Call on the sun its course to stay,
Think'st thou it heeds? Then Love makes moan,
Left in the ambushed hush alone,

Beleaguered with secret fears about,
To battle with Amoritish doubt:
For O, my moon of Ajalon! see,
The lance that pierces the blazonry
Is *blue*; — it has shotten the crimson pane —

AUGUSTA.

Miserly haggler over the wane
Of a bit of a minute!

ALBRECHT.

But think how few
These minutes! No marvel I seem a Jew,
Exorbitant, grasping, when for gold
I count thy smiles my florins, and hold
Each savour'd word as the sacring-bread
On which my worshipping heart is fed.
And now, while the starveling for a space
Feasts on the sanctity of thy face,
Tell me what hope thou bringest; I wait
Breathless, to learn the drift of fate.

AUGUSTA.

Ah, me! — and the hope is a pallid fear!
But stand we apart by the pillar here

Where the shadows deepen: (My maidens stay
My coming beside the cloister-way
A moment, as I have bidden, there
To wait, as they deem, my one last prayer:)
  But the tidings?—Yea. Thou knowest, I wis,
How stern of speech, and how strong of will,
  And how haughty of mien my father is.
Well—yesternight in a softer mood
  He seemed, as he sate and stroked my hair,
  And likened me to my mother,—fair
He said, as a violet of the wood:
And he praised the picture he bade thee paint
  Of this same brown head; and he laughed anon,
  And vowed when an age or twain had gone,
Church-folk would christen it for a saint,
With its pleading eyes,—and hence, some day,
It might come to pass that men would pray
Before it as Santa Augusta—

ALBRECHT.

One
Kneeleth already—(my shrinèd nun!)

AUGUSTA.

Still praising my mother, he said, her life
Turned on one pivot,—as daughter, wife,

To render *obedience,* instant, true:
He stressed the word; and at once I knew
(For it came with a sudden flash and heat)
That somewhere, a snare was underfeet.
Scared and a-flutter to slip the gin
Ere that its meshes should net me in,
Not meaning it yet, but to forefend
The hidden hazard that might impend,
  I blurted our secret:—How it came
That sitting together day by day
  (The portrait he asked for, all our aim)
And lifting mine eyes to thine alway,
  As artist-wise thou hadst willed, there grew,
Unconscious as grow the buds of May,
  A blossoming love betwixt us two,
Unwatered by spoken word. . . . He flung
My hand from his, as if it had stung,
Just there, to the quick: a wrack of pain
Seized me; but lest I should fear again
To plead, I caught in my palms his face,
And I kissed and I kissed his anger down,
And held, as in leash, the snarling frown
That sprang as I spake to the smile's old place,
Thus bribing my way the sweet tale through.

ALBRECHT.

High-hearted and leal and brave and true —

AUGUSTA.

Nay, hear to the end: I charged that *he*
(As if, lest the seed ungermed remain)
Had showered opportunity, as the rain,
When from thine etchings he summoned thee,
Reluctant, to deck his banquet-hall,
Linking, perforce, our daisied hours
Into a chain of mystic flowers,
While to my hands commending all.
Once, as I paused for breath, he flung
His tankard of wine upon the floor;
I saw that his rage was foaming o'er —

ALBRECHT.

(For me — for *me* was the dear heart wrung!)

AUGUSTA.

But I gave no heed; and I made him know
Ambition had set thy soul aflame;
I pointed to Leonardo: so
Thou too shouldst stand as a prince, — thy name

On the lips of kings, and their guest, as he, —
That even a Baron might grow to be
Proud . . . *There* he stopped me: — and then he swore
A terrible oath I quailed before,
That never, henceforth, should I see thee more.

ALBRECHT.

O love, thou wilt dare his wrath? — thou hast!

AUGUSTA.

Yea, — only to tell thee all is past, —
Is past, — and we meet in the crowd no more
Just to touch hands, as heretofore,
After our vesper prayer. Yet who
May measure what chance and change can do?
And the waiting-time, — will it seem so long
To hearts that are loving and young and strong
And trustful as ours? — But hark! I hear
The clatter of hoofs at the great east door;
. . . What if my father —

ALBRECHT.

Sweetheart, fear
Sharpens thy sense: 'Tis nothing more

Than some Nurembergers hot with wine,
  Who trouble the street with noisy fray:
But here for a moment at Sebald's shrine
  Kneel, till I banish thy dread away.

—Out from the dim cathedral Albrecht passed,
And scanned the Platz where burghers came and went,
And crimson-bodic'd maidens laughed 'good-night,'
Flinging out kisses in their wasteful way,
And children gambolled: but he nowhere saw
The angry father with his men-at-arms
(As on his daughter's frighted fancy flashed),
Waiting to snatch her thence, and hide her where
The 'arrogant smith' should never find her. Then
Turning, a grasp detained him, and he knew
The Baron's chaplain, who had questionings
Touching some altar-panel. Albrecht failed
To shake him off, nor dared to leave him, lest
Following, he should know all. Thus held, he heard
A smothered call. Back through the dusking aisles
He rushed amain,—only to catch the gleam
Of a white garment, at the farther door,—
Only to hear, outside the walls, the hoofs
Of galloping horsemen swallowed in the gloom.

— Never again in Nuremberg was seen
The Baron's daughter. None could surely tell
If walled in convent-cloisters, she dragged on
Her death-in-life; or, if the hapless bride
Of some rude lord, in solitude she starved
Her heart, and died so. Albrecht's dream was dreamed:
No other love profaned his soul's pure shrine
Through his half century's years: — and each rapt face
That grew henceforth beneath his hand, was only
Augusta, with the halo round her hair.[8]

EMIGRAVIT.

(Inscribed on the tomb of Albrecht Dürer, at Nuremberg.)

I.

WELL was it written: Three hundred years grown hoary
With old-world life, have lichened o'er his head,
Since here was traced the simple legend-story
Of him they mourned, — not dead,
Only gone hence, they said.

II.

The Oread winds of each Franconian mountain,
The antique city where they nurse his fame, —
First of possessions, — dome and arch and fountain
Are vital with the claim
Wherewith they hoard his name.

III.

Wherever Art hath borne her smallest treasure,
Wherever Beauty's worship hath a place,
His praise is spoken in yet richer measure,
Than to his living face
They ever spake his praise.

IV.

Truth, with severe yet earnest justice, holds him
Close to her breast. Religion, on his brow
Setting her kiss, with shielding arms enfolds him,
His service to avow,
Her Art-priest then and now.

V.

For he did teach the ages adoration
Of all things holy. His so hallowed skill
Came to the people like a revelation,
Divine, yet human still,
Interpreting God's will.

VI.

His Gothic fancy widened Art's dominions;
His freer instincts rent the clogs away,
Wherewith old forms had cobwebbed the strong pinions
That courted sweep and sway
Through purer faith's full day.

VII.

And so, because he wrought the lore whose lessons
Take hold on heaven, and stretch to grasp the sky,—
Because his burin breathes the immortal essence
That time and death defy,
Therefore he cannot die.

VIII.

Well then it hath been written of Albrecht Dürer,
  Through all the centuries drifting o'er his head, —
Those centuries that but make his fame securer,
    The Master is not dead,
    Only gone hence, they said.

MURILLO'S TRANCE.

"Here, Pedro, while I quench these candles, hold
My lantern; for, I promise you, we burn
No waxlights at our chapel-shrines till morn,
As in the great Cathedral, kept ablaze
Like any crowded plaza in Seville,
From sun to sun. I wonder if they think
That the dead knights, — Fernando and the rest, —
Whose bronze and marble couches line the walls,
Like to scared children, cannot sleep i' the dark:"
And, muttering thus, the churlish Sacristan
Went, snuffing out the lights that only served
To worsen the wan gloom.
                                        And (mindful still
Of his Dolores' greed of candle-ends)
He chid, at whiles, some lagging worshipper,
Nor spared to hint, above the low-dropp'd heads,
Grumblings of sunshine being in Seville
Cheaper than waxlight, and 'twere best to pray

When all the saints were broad awake, and thus
Liker to hear.
So shuffling on, he neared
The altar with its single lamp a-light.
Above, touched with its glow, the chapel's pride,
Its one Ribéra hung, — a fearful-sad,
Soul-harrowing picture of the stark dead Christ,
Stretcht on the cross beneath a ghastly glare
Of lurid rift, that made more terrible
The God-forsaken loneliness. In front,
A chasm of shadow clove the checker'd floor,
And hastening towards it, the old verger called
Wonderingly back:
"Why, Pedro, only see!
The boy kneels still! What ails him, think you? Here
He came long hours before the vesper-chime;
And all the while, as to and fro I've wrought, —
Cleansing of altar-steps and dusting shrines,
And such like tasks, I have not missed him once
From that same spot. What marvel if he were
Some lunatic escaped from *Caridad?*
Observe! he takes no heed of aught I say:
'Tis time he waked."
As moveless as the statues

Niched round, a youth before the picture knelt,
His hands tight clenched, and his moist forehead strewn
With tossings of dank hair. Upon his arm
The rude old man sprang such a sudden grasp
As caused a start; while in his ear he cried
Sharply, "Get hence! What do you here so late?"

Slow on the questioner a face was turned
That caused the heavy hand to drop; a face
Strangely pathetic, with wide-gazing eyes
And wistful brows, and lips that wanly made
Essay to speak before the words would come;
And an imploring lifting of the hands
That seemed a prayer:
—"*I wait,—I wait,*" he said,
"*Till Joseph bring the linen, pure and white,*
Till Mary fetch the spices; till they come,
Peter and John and all the holy women,
And take Him down; but O, they tarry long!
See how the darkness grows! So long, . . . so long!"

THE SHADOW.

Day by day, through morns of misted splendor;
Under noons that brought
Breathless languors; into twilights tender,
Still the artist wrought;

Striving through his pencil's skilled expression,
Forth to lure the train
Of the haunting beings, whose procession
Trooped athwart his brain.

In the tumult of creative passion,
Sometimes there would come
Quickening throes of so supreme a fashion,
That the flesh sank dumb

In the presence of their revelations,
Uttering no complaint,
Though the rending pain of such creations
Left it weak and faint.

Yet not always was the spirit master;
    And one day, there grew,
As Velasquez labored fast and faster,
    Feud betwixt the two.

Just a touch, — and in its finished beauty
    Would his picture shine,
Setting forth a deed of lowly duty,
    Till it seemed divine.

But irresolute the painter pondered,
    With a brow perplexed,
And distrustfully his vision wandered,
    And his voice grew vext.

"Ah, that shadow! Why, the water bickered
    Here but yesterday;
Now, the sheeny light that o'er it flickered,
    Fades to rusty gray.

"See! this flesh has lost its vital shimmer;
    Here, all radiance dies;
Strange! I cannot find one living glimmer
    In those staring eyes!

"Let me sweep my canvas of such creatures!"
And with passion's rush,
As he raised his hand to dash the features,
With full-laden brush, —

From behind a grasp his act arrested:
"Are you mad? Behold!
To confirm your picture's worth attested,
Here be bags of gold,

"Which the king has sent as payment proffered,
Should you choose it so;
More than double what Don Luis offered
Just three days ago.

"*Shadow?* Why, I shrivel in yon torrid
Blaze of tropic light,
And unwittingly I shield my forehead,
Lest it blind my sight.

"Get you forth mid Andalusian meadows,
For I hold it plain
Nature's turning on you, — casting shadows
Over eye and brain.

"Give her respite, or may come disaster
Which you dare not brave;
For she will not, though she owns you master,
Stoop to be your slave.

"Spirit goads the flesh, and like the Prophet,
Urges left and right,
Past the hindering shadow: Do not scoff it,
Lest the angel smite."

TINTORETTO'S LAST PAINTING.*

I.

O BITTER, bitter truth! I see it now,
  Heightening the lofty calmness of her face,
Until it seems transfigured: On her brow
  The gray mists settle. I begin to trace
The whitening circle round her lips; the fine
Curve of the nostril pinches, . . . ah, the sign
Indubitable! I dare thrust aside
No longer what ye oft in vain have tried
To force upon my sight, that day by day
My Venice-lily drops her leaves away,
  While I have seen no fading, — I, who should
    Have known it earliest.

II.

Only thirty years
For this unfolding flush of womanhood
  To fruiten into ripeness: O, if tears

* The portrait of his artist-daughter, Marietta Robusti, as she lay dying.

Could bribe, how soon my harvested fourscore
  Should take the thirty's place! For I have had
Life's large ingathering, and I crave no more.
  But she, . . . she just begins to taste how glad
The mellower clusters are, — when see! — the woe!
  One blast of mortal ravage, and here lies
    Before my startled eyes,
The laden vine, uprooted at a blow.

III.

My *Paradiso* * does not hold a face
  That is not richer through my darling's gift:
  One angel has the hushed, adoring lift
Of her arched lids; another wears the grace
  That dimples round her flexile mouth; and one
  — The nearest to The Mother and her Son —
  Borrows the tawny glory of her hair:
And yet, — how strange! — as full and perfect whole,
Her form, her features, all the breathing soul
  Of her, I have not pictured otherwhere.

IV.

Tommàso, bring my colors hither: Haste!
    We have no time to waste.

* Tintoretto's master-piece.

Draw back the curtain; in the fairest light
Set forth my easel, — I am blind to-night,
  Blind through my weeping. But I must not lose
Even the shadow's shadow. Now they prop
  Her for the breeze: There! just as I would choose,
They smooth the pillows. Dear Ottavia, drop
  Your Persian scarf across her couch, that so
Its wine-red flecks may interfuse the cold
  Blanch of the linen's deaded snow.

V.

Nay, — hold!
Give her no hint; forbear to let her know
That the old doting father fain would snatch
  This phantom from death's grip. My child! my child!
  My inmost soul rebels, unreconciled!
Heart sinks, hand palsies, while I strive to match
  Such beatific loveliness with blot
Of earthly color. All my tints but seem
Ashen and muddy to reflect the gleam
  Of those celestial eyes fast-fixt on what
Spirits alone can see. Ah! now, — she smiles —

VI.

Look on my canvas: if the wish beguiles
Not judgment, I have caught a glimmer here

Of the old shine that used to flash so clear
  Across our evening circle, — like the last
Long sunset ray aslant our gray lagunes,
  When she would lean, with Veronese anear,
Beside the sill, and listen to the tunes
  Of gondoliers who 'neath our windows passed.
Now softly bid Ottavia loosen out
  Her golden-thridded hair; and bring a rose
  From yonder vase, and let her fingers close,
— Poor, fragile fingers! — the green stem about.

VII.

Yea, — so! But all is blurred through rush of tears:
  Only the vanish'd, mocking long ago,
Frescoed with memories of her happy years,
  Betwixt me and the canvas seems to glow.
                And now, — and now!
  Her hair rays off, — an aureole round her brow:
  And see! Tommàso, see! I understand
  Not what I do: for, in her slackening hand,
I've put a palm-branch where I meant the rose
  Should drop its spark of warmth the whiteness o'er;
How wan she looks! Surely the pallor grows, —
  Nay, push the easel back, . . . I can no more!

WOMAN'S ART.

(In Bologna.)

More than three hundred years ago
(Hunt for the place where it tells you so
There in your Baedeker), lived and wrought,
Here in Bologna, a girl, whose thought,
Carved on the stone of a plum, survives
The volumed records of thousand lives.

Yes, you were shown the frieze, you say,
In San Petronio, the other day,
And the pair of angels that bear her name
Properzia, — marvellous works these same,
Being a woman's. But did you know,
Praising the antique cuttings so,
  Who made them? Maestro Amico,
Her artist-neighbor, refused to see
Rareness in any work that she,
A woman, might plan. "A woman's power
Bends to the sway of the passing hour;

Achieves, but never creates. The stone
Of the quarries was meant for men alone,
Whose genius had gift to shape it: walls
Of churches, basilicas, palace-halls,
Only were ample enough to yield
To limitless skill, the nobler field:
But woman! . . . a cherry-stone might well
Hold whatsoever *she* had to tell!"

Misprized and taunted, the maiden's pride
Would none of the marble thus denied,
Nor the canvas grudged. Henceforth she wrought
On the kernel of olive and apricot,
Marvels of frost-like carvings, — such
As grew under Benvenuto's touch.
Go to the Casa Grassi: see
The scene of the Passion on Calvary:
Mark, as you may, the sacred head,
And the Godlike look o'er the features shed,
And honor the art that skilled to trace
Such miracles scarce in an inch's space.

Now puzzle the guide by asking where
Are the wonderful frescoes, vast and rare,

Of her neighbor, the jealous artist, who
Flung her his scorn. . . . Just so! I knew
His name would be strange to the Bolognese:
— Did ever it reach *us*, over seas?

Yet woman is weak for Art, you prove,
Since her genius works in a narrow groove;
But if, as the crucial test appears,
It ever outlives three hundred years,
Better thus work than chafe or starve,
— Give her the plum-stone and let her carve!

FROM THE LIFE

OF THE

LEGENDS.

ST. GREGORY'S SUPPER.

I.

"SERVANT *of servants:** that is the name
Falleth the fittest when they call;
Jesus, my Master, bore the same,
Even though sovereign Lord of all.
Shut in my crypt by night, by day,
Breathing His peace with every breath,
I was content to wear away,
Tasting a calm as sweet as death:
Yet they have bidden me forth to bear
Mitre and cope and sacred staff, —
Burdens that stoop my heart with care, —
Heart that is weak as winnowed chaff.

II.

"Valens, abide with me, friend of friends,
Share, as we use, the weal, the woe:

* *Servus Servorum*, — St. Gregory's chosen title.

Order my household, make amends,
  Steading me thus, to poor and low,
Whom, in their hovels I'll see no more.
  Gather each night about my board
Twelve gray beggars to halve my store;
  (Am I not almoner for my Lord?)
Twelve of the outcasts: even to such
  Still I would Servant of servants be;
Small the abasement; think how much
  Lower the Master stooped for me."

III.

Forth to his service the Pontiff passed,
  Wrapt in his prayerful thoughts apart,
Watchful lest clouding pride should cast
  Shadows of bale above his heart.
Valens made haste against he came,
  Summoned as guests the twelve he bade,
Hungry and homeless, vile of name,
  Only in filth and rags arrayed:
Just as they were, defiled, unsweet,
  Grimed with the squalid scurf of sin,
Pressing their hands their host did greet
  Each, as they wondering entered in.

IV.

Lifting his voice he prayed, then brake
  Generous bread for their free repast:—
"Welcome," he said, "for the dear Lord's sake;"
  While on the group his eyes he cast.
"As it is written: *He sat at meat* .
  Thus with the Twelve:—Ha! what may it mean?
Valens, I bade that but *twelve* should eat,
  Yet there be verily here, *thirteen!*"
Valens made answer: "Even so,
  Heeded I, hearkening to thy hest;
One hath intruded, nor do I know
  Wherefore he sitteth among the rest."

V.

"Whence art thou come unbidden?—speak!"
  Straightway the stranger then gave reply:
"Once did a way-worn palmer seek
  Alms of thee, passing thy cloister by;
'Nothing,' (thou said'st,) 'is mine to give,
  Saving this silvern bowl,—to me
Gift of my mother: yet take, and live.'
  —Know'st thou the palmer? *I am he!*"

Ev'n as he spake his face waxed faint,
  Brightened and passed in a splendor dim,
Leaving them mazed; and then the Saint
  Knew it was Christ who had supped with him!

DOROTHEA'S ROSES.

(IN FLORENCE.)

YES, here is the old cathedral ;
  Out of the glare and heat,
We'll plunge in these depths of coolness,
  (Take the *prie-dieu* for a seat):

Bathe in this gloom your vision
  So tired with frescoed shows,
And let the slow ripples of silence,
  Tide-like, around you close.

Then at your ease I'll show you
  That picture of Carlo's,* — the sight
Of whose so ineffable sweetness,
  Prismed my dreams last night.

* Carlo Dolce's *St. Dorothea.*

Surely you've heard the legend
  — Saint Cyprian hands it down —
Of the beautiful Dorothea,
  Who was crowned with the fiery crown?

No? Then sit as you're sitting
  There, in that oaken stall,
Just where the great rose-window
  Splendors the eastern wall, —

Just where the sunset shivers
  Its darts on the altar rail,
And while the blue smoke of the incense
  Rises, I'll tell the tale.

There dwelt (while the old religion
  For the languid East sufficed,
While the Grecian Zeus was worshipped
  In the temples instead of Christ, —

When burnings and rack and dungeon
  Awaited the neophyte
Who turned from an idol's statue,
  Or shrank from a pagan rite),

In a fair Greek city, a maiden
  Whose praises were noised abroad
Because of her wondrous beauty,
  And they called her *The Gift of God.*

One day as she passed, bestowing
  Oblations at Herè's shrine,
Strange words to her ear were wafted,
  New doctrines that seemed divine:

And, pausing, she listened. The hermit
  Placed in her hands a scroll,
— Saint John-the-Divine's sweet Gospel;
  She read, — and believed the whole.

Henceforth in the faith of her fathers,
  No longer the maiden trod;
She kneeled at a purer altar,
  And worshipped the Christians' God.

Thereat did the fierce proconsul
  Rise in his wrath: "Deny
This myth of the Galilean,
  Or thou, by the gods, shalt die!"

Meekly she bowed before him,
With a trust no threat could dim:
"He hath died for *me*, and I cannot,
I dare not do less for *Him!*"

As out through the gates of the city
They led her to meet her death,
From the midst of his gay companions,
Hilarion, mocking, saith:

"Ha! goest thou, lovely maiden,
(Such joy on thy face I see),
Afar to some fair Elysium,
Where thy bridegroom awaiteth thee?

"If there an Hesperides' garden
Blooms that is brighter than ours,
Send me, beseech thee, in token,
A spray of celestial flowers."

She smiled with a smile seraphic:
"Is *that* of thy faith the price?
Then, verily, thou shalt have roses
Gathered in Paradise!"

Onward she went exulting,
  As though she were borne mid-air,
And lo! as she neared the pyre,
  A fair-haired boy stood there, —

In his hand, three dewy roses
  Clustered about their stem:
"Ah! hasten," she said, "sweet angel,
  Hilarion waits for them!"

. . . . .

Come now and see Carlo's picture
  Of the maiden as she stands
With the golden nimbus around her,
  And the roses within her hands.

FRANCESCA'S WORSHIP.

In the deep afternoon, when westering calms
Brooded above the streets of Rome, and cooled
Their sultry clamor, at her orisons
In San Domenico, Francesca knelt.

All day her charities had overflowed
For others. Husband, children, friends, had claimed
Service ungrudged. The poor had found their wage
Doubled by reason of her soothing hands:
Sick eyes had lifted at her step, as lifts
The parcht Campagna grass at the cool kiss
Of winds that have been dallying with the snows
Of Alban mountain-tops. And now, released
From outward ministries, and free to turn
Inward, and up the solemn aisle of thought
Conduct her soul, she bowed with open page
Before the altar: "*Tenuisti manum*
Dexteram meam" —

On her lips she held
The words distillingly, as though she drained
A honeyed drop from each slow syllable;
But even while her whisper clove the air
Upon her still seclusion breaking, came
A messenger:
"Sweet mistress, grace, I pray!
But, unaware, our lord hath come again,
Guests at his back; and he hath bidden me fetch
My lady, if for only one half-hour,
Saying, the wine was flavorless without
Her hand to pour it."
At the word she rose,
And unreluctant went. No undertow
Of secret fret disturbed th' unrippled blue
Of those serenest eyes that mirrored heaven.
Then, when they all had been refreshed, and forth
Had ridden abroad, Francesca sought her place
Before the shrine. The refluent wave of prayer,
Held in brief poise by duty's interclaim,
Bore back her soul into a tideless calm,
As o'er the Psalter's leaf again she pored:
—"*In voluntate tua deduxisti*"—
She conned it with an iterating joy,

As though she heard the voice drop through the fringe
Of angel-faces frescoed round the dome.
So tranced, she caught no footfall on the floor,
Nor knew that any spake, until there fell
A quiet touch:
"The Sister Barbara
Comes seeking wherewithal to dress some wounds
Got in a brawl upon the Appian Way."

And now athwart the western windows gleamed
Rainbows of shafted light, as thither, back
Francesca came to end her "Offices."
A ray, that seemed a burnished pencil held
Within the fingers of the Christ that glowed
In the stained oriel, pointed to the words
Where she had paused, to do the nun's behest:
"*Cum gloria suscepisti me.*" She kissed
The illumined leaf, thanks nestling at her heart,
That here, at last, no duty disallowing,
Her loosened soul out through the sunset bars
Might float, and catch heaven's crystal sheen. But scarce
Had meditation smoothed the wing of thought,
Before the hangings of the door unclosed
With yet a further summons. From a Triton
That spouted in the court, her three-year boy,

Through wayward prank, had fallen; and naught would soothe
The lacerate brow save the soft mother-kiss.

"I come," she said, her forehead luminous
With inward light: "For Thou wouldst teach me, Lord,
That Thou art just as near me, ministering
At home, as in these consecrated aisles;
And that I worship Thee as purely, when
I pour the wine for him I love, or hold
The little throbbing head, as when I bow
Above the sacred leaf, — since duty's shrine
Is the true altar where I serve Thee best."

When under the Campagna's purple rim
The sun had sunk so long that all was gray,
Once more across the dusking sacristy
Francesca glided back. The Psalter lay
Scarcely discernible amid the gloom;
But lo, the marvel! On the open page,
The verse which thrice she had essayed to read,
Now shone irradiate, silver-clear, as though
God's hand had written it with the flash of stars!

THE BISHOP'S BAN.

(A Legend of St. Ambrose.)

Upon his staff the holy man
  Leaned, girt for journeying:
"But, ere I get me hence," he bade,
  "Beseech ye, hither bring
My one-night host, to whom behooves,
  I speak a certain thing."

Then straightway came the baron forth,
  To whom the bishop said:
"I and my hungry acolytes,
  With travel-toil bestead,
Since yester-eve have been refreshed
  Through breaking of thy bread.

"And now, what wilt thou? Is there naught
  That I, our Lord, his thrall,

Through prayer may win for thee, what time
  On Jesu Christ I call?
No holier joys, no richer stores
  Than yet to thee befall?"

Then lightly laughed the Tuscan knight:
  "Good Milan Bishop, grace!
Bestow thy prayer some otherwhere;
  No alms beseem my case:
Nor yet withal for ghostly gifts
  Find I a hand-breadth's place.

"A brave, right winsome world is this,
  That stints not of its store:
No sickness have I known, — my heart
  Was never sorrow-sore:
The Church's benison, I wis,
  Would fail to bring me more.

"No wife in all our Tuscany,
  I swear, is fair as mine;
No ruddier children dance away
  Sunsetting 'neath the vine;
And, at my feast of life, friends' talk
  Is sweet as parsley'd wine.

" My lands have broadened till they reach
  Yon gray-green brede of sea:
My wains are burdened with their sheaves,
  So vast my harvests be;
And liefly, mine own vassal folk
  Do yield their fealty.

" Strong manhood's doughty lustiness
  Riots in every vein:
Go to, Sir Bishop! what have I
  At thy wan hands to gain?
Keep thou thy heaven, and I, my earth, —
  At best, till age and pain — "

" Hold! hold thy scoffs!" St. Ambrose cried;
  " Friends, hie ye all a-field,
Nor tarry near this roof foredoomed,
  For to mine eyes revealed,
I read: *Thou hast thy good things here!*
  The sentence signed and sealed."

Forth gat the frighted acolytes,
  Forth gat the Bishop gray,

Without the gates: and nevermore
  Did any from that day
See aught, where rose the castle walls,
  But piles that ruined lay.

CONSUMMATUM EST.

(A.D. 735.)

SCRIPTOR.

THOU art weary, Father: Rest,
While I bear the scrolls away
Till some morrow's stronger day,
For the sun drops down the west,
Near to setting—

ST. BEDE.

Surely so,—
Near to setting: Therefore dip
Quicklier still thy pen and write
What my strength may yet indite,
Ere dead silence ash my lip,
And my holiest work forego
Full completion.

SCRIPTOR.

There remains
But one chapter of St. John,

Ere the whole be overgone ;
So, beseech thee, pause : thy pains
Wrack thee :

ST. BEDE.

Ah, my Saxons ! they
Must have Christ's full gospel : Pray
Haste the transcript — haste it.

SCRIPTOR.

Yea,
As thou wilt then.

. . . .

Father, now
Just one verse till — *Selah :* (How
Fast the dark creeps !) See ! 'tis done :

ST. BEDE.

Consummatum est ; my son,
Thou hast said it —

SCRIPTOR.

Ha ! his head
Drops : God's mercy, — he is dead !

BEDA VENERABILIS.

THERE was grief in the quiet cloister,
  One sorrowful Easter day;
For under the chapel pavement
  In tranquillest slumber lay
The gentle and saintly abbot,
  Who had passed in his peace away.

And Wilbert, the clerkly scriptor,
  Who came at the teacher's call,
And day after day had written
  His words, as he heard them fall, —
Wilbert sate bowed with weeping,
  The sorest bereaved of all.

"Now what shall we trace above him,
  Deep-graved in the flag's smooth stone,
Whereby, in the after ages,
  His name shall be fitly known,
Who wrought till his locks all bleachen
  In the service of God had grown?"

And he chose from the stores of vellum,
  A sheet of the fairest white,
(With a sob as he thought of the master,
  Who never would more indite),
And he sate on the ancient settle,
  And dipped his pen to write.

And he wrote: — "*Hâc sunt in fossa* —
  Though the tears would his eyelids brim,
"*Bedæ* — (then a blank line) — *ossa:*"
  What word should be linked with him?
And he pondered, and searched, and questioned,
  Till his puzzled brain grew dim.

For many a night-long vigil
  And fasting had Wilbert kept,
As close by the dying pillow
  He had written, and watched, and wept:
Now, soothed by invisible fingers,
  He slackened his pen, and slept.

And when with a start he wakened
  From the slumber he had not willed,

He found on the clear sheet written
  (And a wonder within him thrilled),
Bedæ VENERABILIS *ossa:*
  —The blank he had left was filled!

RABBI SIMEON'S PARABLE.

And it came to pass as the sun waxed hot,
  And crowds in the synagogue came and went,
  That under an oak they pitched his tent,
    And the Rabbi sat and taught.

And ever and oft as his eyes would stray
  Beyond the circle that girt him round,
  On Lebanon's slopes they rested, — crowned
    With its silvery crown alway;

As along by the brinded belts of green,
  Leading their flocks from rill to rill,
  Up where the grass shone lusher still,
    Were the distant shepherds seen.

Then lifting his voice, the Rabbi spake
  To his young disciples: "Behold ye now,
  Those sheep new-washen, on Horon's brow,
    Each fair as a fresh snow flake;

And mark in their very midst, as well
  Ye wondering may, where quiet as though
  It followed beside the mother-doe,
    There browses a brown gazelle.

"And Imlah the shepherd avoucheth us
  Concerning the dappled thing: One day,
  As it watched from a crag the flocks at play,
    As yonder disporting thus, —

"From its rocky haunts and its bleating dam's
  Udder unweaned, it straightway sped
  Down to the pastured plain, and fed
    As a lamb amidst the lambs.

"And at folding time, when the day is o'er,
  Wild-natured still, and as shy as erst,
  It follows the flock, and is oft-times first
    To enter the wattled door.

"And therefore doth Imlah the shepherd shield
  It even with yet a gentler care,
  Than any his bosom'd weanlings share,
    As he leadeth them all a-field.

"He hath cherished *them* alway; *they* have left
No wilderness mates, — no coverts grown
Wonted by reason of use, alone
To break from their native cleft,

"And join them with strangers. Hearken ye,
Now unto my parable's lesson: God,
Who guideth His chosen with staff and rod,
Where fairest the pastures be, —

"Doth welcome the alien, who to dwell
Among them, all other ties hath riven,
With love that is passing tender, — even
As the shepherd yon brown gazelle."

SAINT MARTIN'S TEMPTATION.

I.

For forty and five long years
  I have followed my Master, Christ;
Through frailty and toils and tears,
  Through passions that still enticed:
Through honors that came unsought,
  To dazzle, ensnare, betray;
Through the baits the Tempter brought
  To lure me out of the way;
Through the peril and greed of power,
  (The bribe that *he* thought most sure!)
Through the name that hath made me cower,
  "The *holy* Bishop of Tours!"
Now, faint with the droil of care,
  I am waiting to enter in
To the only cloister where
  My soul shall be safe from sin.

II.

Ah, none but my Lord hath seen
  How oft I have swerved aside;
How the word or the look serene
  Hath hidden the heart of pride.
When a beggar once crouched in need,
  I flung him my priestly stole,
And the people did laud the deed,
  Withholding, the while, their dole:
  Then I closed my lips on a curse,
  Like a scorpion curled within,
On such cheap charity, — worse
  Was even than theirs, my sin!
And once, when a royal hand
  Brake bread for the Christ's sweet grace;
I was proud that a queen should stand
  And serve in the henchman's place.

III.

But illest of all bestead
  Was a night in my narrow cell
As I pondered with low-bowed head,
  A purpose that pleased me well.

'Twas fond to the sense and fair,
  Attuned to the heart and will,
While yet on its face it bare
  The look of a duty still :
And I murmured, as doubt took wing,
  "Where reason and choice accord,
It is even a pleasant thing
  To the flesh, to serve the Lord!"

IV.

I turned, and I saw a sight
  Wondrous and strange to see,
A being as marvellous bright
  As the visions of angels be:
His vesture was woven of flame,
  And a crown on his forehead shone
With jewels of nameless name,
  Like the glory about the Throne.
"Worship thou me," he said ;
  And I sought as I sank, to trace
Through his hands above me spread,
  The lineaments of his face.
I pored on each palm to see

The scar of the *stigma*, where
They had fastened him to the Tree,
But, — no print of the nails was there!
Then I shuddered, aghast of brow,
As I cried, — "Accurst! abhorred!
Get thee behind me! for thou
Art Satan, and not my Lord!"
He vanished before the spell
Of the Sacred Name I named,
And I lay in my darkened cell,
Repentant, astonied, shamed.
Thenceforth, whatever the dress
That a seeming duty ware,
I knew 'twas a wile, *unless*
The print of the nails was there.

THE REAPERS OF LANDISFARNE.

I.

In his abbey cell Saint Cuthbert
  Sate burdened and care-dismayed:
For the wild Northumbrian people,
  For whom he had wrought and prayed,
Still clung to their warlike pastime,
  Their plunder and border raid;

II.

Still scouted all peaceful tillage,
  And queried with scowling brow,
"Shall we who have won our victual
  By the stout, strong hand till now,
Forswearing the free, bold foray,
  Crawl after the servile plow?"

III.

"Through year and through year I have taught
them,
By the word of my mouth," he said;
"And still, in their untamed rudeness,
They trust to the wilds for bread;
But now will I teach henceforward,
By the toil of my hands instead.

IV.

"In their sight I will set the lesson;
And, gazing across the tarn,
They shall see on its nether border,
Garth, byre, and hurdled barn,
And the brave, fair field of barley
That shall whiten at Landisfarne."

V.

Therewith from his Melrose cloister
Saint Cuthbert went his way:
He felled the hurst, and the meadow
Bare him rich swaths of hay,
And forth and aback in the furrow
He wearied the longsome day.

VI.

And it came to pass when the autumn
The ground with its sere leaves strawed,
And the purple was over the moorlands,
And the rust on the sunburnt sod,
That ripe for the reaper, the barley
Silvered the acres broad.

VII.

Then certain among the people,
Fierce folk who had laughed to scorn
The cark of the patient toiler,
While riot, and hunt, and horn,
Were wiling them in the greenwood,
Cried: "Never Northumbrian born,

VIII.

"Shall make of his sword a sickle,
Or help to winnow the heap:
The hand that hath sowed may garner
The grain as he list, — or sleep,
And pray the hard Lord he serveth,
That His angels may come and reap."

IX.

Right sadly Saint Cuthbert listened;
And, bowing his silvered head,
He sought for a Christ-like patience
(As he lay on his rush-strewn bed),
And strength for the morrow's scything,
Till his fears and his sadness fled.

X.

Then he dreamed that he saw descending
On the marge of the moorland tarn,
A circle of shining reapers,
Who heaped in the low-eaved barn,
The sheaves that their gleaming sickles
Had levelled at Landisfarne.

XI.

In the cool of the crispy morning,
Ere the lark had quitted her nest
In the beaded grass, the sleeper
Arose from his place of rest;
"For," he sighed, "I must toil till the gloaming
Is graying the golden west."

XII.

He turned to look at his corn-land ;
  Did he dream ? Did he see aright ?
— Close cut was the field of barley,
  And the stubble stood thick in sight :
For the reapers with shining sickles
  Had harvested all the night !

THE HERMIT'S VIGIL.

HERE is the ancient legend I was reading
  From the black-letter vellum page, last night:
Its yellow husk holds lessons worth the heeding,
  If we unfold it right.

The tome is musty with dank superstition,
  From which we shrink recoiling to th' extreme
Of an unfaith, that, with material vision,
  Accounts as myth or dream,

Problems too subtle for our clumsy fingers,
  High truths that burn beyond our reach, as far
As o'er the fire-fly in the grass that lingers,
  Burns yonder quenchless star.

Give rather back the old hallucinations, —
The ecstasies, the transport, terror, grief,
Of faith so human, than the drear negations
Of dumb, dead unbelief!

But hear the story now:
Within a forest,
By black morasses girt, a hermit dwelt:
And as one midnight, when the storm raged sorest,
In his lone hut he knelt,

In ghostly penance, sounds of fiendish laughter
Smote on the tempest's lull with hideous jar
That sent the gibbering echoes pealing after,
Through windy wolds afar.

"Christ bring ye ban!" he cried, the door wide flinging;
"Speed ye some whither with perdition's dole?"
"We go" (from out the wrack, a shriek came ringing)
"To seize the emperor's soul,

"Who lies this hour death-stricken." Execration
Thereat, still fouler filled the sulphurous air:
Before the rood the hermit sank: "Salvation
Grant, Lord, in his despair!"

And agonizing thus, with lips all ashen,
He prayed; till back, with ghastlier rage and roar,
The dæmon rout rushed, strung to fiercer passion,
And crashed his ozier door.

"Speak, fiend! I do adjure thee! Came repentance
Too late?" With hissing curse was answer made:
"Heaped high within the Judgment-Scales for sentence,
The emperor's sins were laid;

"And downward, downward, with a plunge descended
Our scale till we exulted, — when a moan,
— '*Save, Christ, O, save me!*' — from his lips was rended
Out with his dying groan.

"Quick in the other scale did Mercy lay it,
Lo! *it outweighed his guilt* — "
"Ha, baffled! braved!"
The hermit cried; "Hence, fiends! nor dare gainsay it,
The emperor's soul is saved!"

BACHARACH WINE.

(A.D. 1494.)

I.

"Why should they crown *me* Emperor? Why
Summon me hither from merry cheer
With my life-long wassailers? Surely I,
Prince of good fellows, am happier here.
I smother to think of the cramping weight
Of Charlemagne's iron about my brow:
My own Bohemia's crown and state
Are more than enough for me, I vow,
When I'd cast off care, and drink my full
Of wine and wit at the Königstuhl.

II.

"I wonder if Charlemagne ever drank
A tankard of Assmanshausen? Nay,
If he had, his empire never would rank
As it does with the royalest realms to-day.

For the goddess that laughs within the cup,
  Had wiled and won him from blood and war,
And shown, as he drained her long draughts up,
  There was something better worth living for
Than kingcraft, keeping his gruff brow sad;
  (— I wish from my very soul she had!)

III.

"Consider now, Rupert! With such a realm
  As that to govern from year to year;
The brain must be steady that holds the helm,
  The senses alert and quick and clear.
And how could I dare to jest and drink,
  Till brain grew dizzy, and sense a wrack?
For I never would be the man, I think,
  To shirk the burden once on my back:
But what's an Imperial name, I pray,
  To the madness of drinking the soul away?

IV.

"This Assmanshausen! Why, I declare,
  There never was such heart-staying wine,
So brimmed with the sky, the sun, the air,
  Vintaged along our lordly Rhine —"

8

"I challenge thy word," Prince Rupert said;
  "I know a better by seven-fold,
With a century's warp of cobwebs spread
  Over the barrels mossed and old.
He never has been to heaven and back,
  Who has not drunken of Bacharach."

V.

"Now by my sceptre," roared the King,
  "Fetch me the wine thus held so high,
And if it can *twice* the rapture bring
  That slumbers in Assmanshausen — why,
Here on the spot I'll lay thee down,
  (Inly thou cravest it now, I trow,)
Plighted and pledged, the Iron crown:
  Hasten! — a flagon! — let me know
At once if this Bacharach can be
  More than an Emperor's state to me."

VI.

The wine was brought him, — the bowls were filled,
  And they drank deep into the winter night,
Till the heart of the new-made Emperor thrilled,
  And tingled with such divine delight,

That he cried: "Prince Rupert, if thou wilt give
  Three butts a year of Bacharach wine,
Just such as this, through the years I live,
  Then Charlemagne's sceptre shall be thine."
Prince Rupert sware: For his royal guest,
  Freedom and Bacharach wine were best.

THE QUEEN'S KISS.

Upon the purple dais sate the Queen,
Blanche of Castile; and, at her fair right hand,
The Prince, upon whose one decade even then
There dawned a somewhat of the saintlihood
That through the centuries since, still stars his name.
In waiting, pages stood, of noblest rank,
Attent to win, through courtly service wrought,
Those knightliest honors held a prize so high.
Among them one seemed diverse from the rest,
Apart and sad; and his too level gaze
Lacked youth's forecasting eagerness, as though
He reached no hand to pluck at future joy.

The royal glance swept round the hall, and paused
Upon the stranger, who but late had come
Into the household; and the queenly heart,
Instinct with motherhood, leaped forth to meet
The pathos in his face.

"Hence, little Prince,"
She bade, "and bring yon stripling to my knee."
With courtesies, the pledge of breeding had
'Neath palace roofs, the boy knelt at the däis,
And lifted to his lips the broidered hem
Of the Queen's robe, as she besought his name.
He clasped his hands, and with an upward look
Of reverence, softly said: "*I am Prince Hubert,*
Son of Elizabeth of Hungary."

With startled gesture rose the Queen, her eyes
Hazed through quick-coming tears, and lifted up
The kneeling boy.
"*Sancta Elisabetta!*
Thou hadst a blessèd mother! Tell me where
She used to kiss thee."
With a sudden flush
Flooding the day-break whiteness of his face,
He laid his finger where the delicate line
Of eyebrows met. Then framing in her hands
His girl-like cheeks, and solemnly as though
She touched some hallowed reliquaire, the Queen

Kissed over and over again the spot; and fast
His thick sobs rose, as to her passionate prayer
He listened; for upon his shut lids fell
What seemed the dropping of his mother's tears.

THE LEGEND OF THE WOODPECKER.

(A NORWEGIAN TRADITION.)

O'ER a firwood trencher the housewife bent,
With bare arms kneading the barley bread:
And her eyes to the path oft wandering went,
That down to the Fïord led.

"He is late: no boat in the offing yet;
My loaf will be brown as a pine-tree cone,"
She muttered with peevish fume and fret,
As she heated the baking-stone.

Anon at the door a knock was heard;
And out in the gloaming clear and keen,
In well-worn mantle of lynx-skin furred,
Was a shivering traveller seen.

Out-stretching his frost-pinched palm, he spake,
"For the love of God, a bit of dough,
Now lay on the hearth for me and bake;"
And ashamed to say him — *No*,

A miserly morsel the kneader chose,
And as in her hand it moulded lay,
A-sudden it spread, and swelled, and rose,
Till it covered the kneading-tray.

"Nay, — here is too much:" and she rolled a piece
Like a curlew's egg: but, as quick as thought,
It overran with its strange increase,
The table at which she wrought.

"See! *this* shall suffice!" she cried, and then,
Choosing what lightly an acorn-cup
Might carry, she shapened it: lo, again
It grew to an armful up.

"Beshrew thee!" she flashed, and her cheek waxed bright
As her crimson cap: "Nor great, nor small
Be any the loaf bestowed to-night,
My Oldsen and I keep all!"

Then sternly the wayfarer chode: "Even though
  Thou hadst more than uttermost need sufficed,
No crumb hath thy greed to give: Now, know,
  The beggar who pleads is — Christ!

"To the doom decreed thee henceforth, hark:
  Thy food, as a bird (from thy kind accurst),
Thou shalt painfully seek 'twixt wood and bark,
          And save when it rains, shalt thirst."

THE COUNT'S SOWING.

I.

OFT had the Abbot of Rudenstein,
  Piously praying within his stall,
Under the castle by the Rhine,
Grudgingly craved the lands whose line
  Bordered his convent garden-wall.

II.

"Long have our fields been far too strait
  For the growing needs of the Brotherhood:
These meadows we'll have or soon or late,
A part and parcel of our estate,
  As sure as there's help in the Holy Rood.

III.

"Lightly will matter an oath or twain,
  If out of it come such good, I trow,
Vellum we have of an ancient stain
Whereon we will write our title plain
  As dated a hundred years ago."

IV.

So mused the Abbot: and in his zeal
  He rated the Count from year to year,
Who heard nor heeded the bold appeal;
For well he reckoned the royal seal
  Whereby he could prove his tenure clear.

V.

But worried and worn by long demand,
  And weakened by hints of churchly threat,
He promised, at length, to yield the land
For ever and aye beneath his hand,
  If one condition were fairly met.

VI.

"Now grant me your leave to sow once more,
  A single crop in the meadows, mine,
The fief of my fathers heretofore;
And, when it is ripe and had in store,
  The soil you covet I thence resign."

VII.

Full gladly the Abbot pledged him true,
  In the Holy Name, all sealed and signed:
The seed it was sown, and the green blades grew
Fast under his eye: but strange to view
  Were the stalks that bent in the waving wind.

VIII.

One day as he watched the field, a groan
  Brake forth as if born of sudden fears;
"Ach Himmel! what hopes are overthrown!
— The crop of acorns the Count hath sown,
  Will not be ripe for a hundred years!"

SAINT LAMBERT'S COAL.

WILD hordes had sacked the minster: scattered
Upon the broken pavement lay
The crash of luminous windows shattered
By lawless hands in wanton fray,
Who wrought their worst, and went their way.

Across pale, pictured saints, rude gashes
Showed where their godless blades had thrust
Profane defiance; with thick ashes
Strewn was the altar, and encrust
Was chalice, pyx and urn with rust.

No light within the lamp was kindled,
No curling incense breathed its fume;
And as the lonely evening dwindled,
Swart shadows chill with ghostly gloom,
Wrapped every niche and shrine and tomb.

Anon athwart the murk came stealing
  Faint floatings of a chanted hymn,
That rolled, gust-blown, from floor to ceiling,
  As slowly a procession dim
  Out of the darkness seemed to swim.

Onward it wended, nor did falter,
  Till, breaking silence, one cried: "Who
Bethought him of the quenchèd altar?
  Alas, how guide the service through?
  Would God might light the lamp anew!"

"*Amen!*" adown the aisle came drifting,
  And from the train outforth there stole
A little acolyth, who lifting
  His surplice-hem, displayed a coal
  That glowed, — yet left the garment whole.

"*Christus Illuminator!*" kneeling,
  The wondering Bishop cried: "From whom
Can light else come? Thyself revealing,
Give forth that faith to chase our gloom,
  Which burns, and yet doth not consume?

"Such faith is thine, O Lambert! Lighten
  Therewith the altar-lamp, and let
Its rays to distant ages brighten."
He took the coal, — the flame reset,
  And there, they tell, 'tis burning yet.

THE LEAVES OF HEALING.

THE fragrant waftings of an old tradition
Come faintly wavering down the world-worn ages,
(Blown from the rosy isle of Aphroditè),

Of Barnabas, who breaking the soft shackles
His Cyprus linked, went far and wide, an exile,
Startling the Greeks with the strange name of Jesus.

And every whither bare he in his bosom
The sacred parchment of St. Matthew's gospel,
Bequeathed him as th' Evangelist lay a-dying.

And when they brought to him, upon his journeys,
The sick, the blind, the palsied, on their foreheads
He laid the writing, and straightway it healed them.

So runs the record; and a hidden meaning
As seed-corn held within a mummy's fingers,
Lies at its core, a germ of living beauty.

For whoso now will bind the holy transcript
Close to his heart, and with a faith as steadfast
As drew the ancient saint from flowery Cyprus,

Will lay upon the soreliest bruisèd spirit,
This medicament, — "*Come unto Me, ye weary,*" —
Its miracle-touch will heal the hurt for ever.

CHRIMHILDE'S TREASURES.

I.

COUNT Conrad sate in his castle tower,
  And leaned his head on his mailèd hands,
As he gazed below on the leaguering foe
  Who battered his walls and spoiled his lands.

II.

"I can do no more: not a crust is left;
  My men lie starved by the donjon keep;
Sweet Chrimhilde alone gives forth no groan,
  As she rocks her boy on her breast asleep.

III.

"If *they* were but saved!" and as he sighed,
  He heard her low footstep on the stair;
And his stout heart bled as he turned his head
  To hide the trace of his blank despair.

IV.

There gleamed a hope in her sunken eye
  As she dropped at his side with a gesture fond,
And sought, in a way that would bide no nay,
  For leave to pass to the hosts beyond.

V.

"Our archers perish: bare ten are left,
  And strengthenless they, to draw the bow;
But, if we must yield, give me thy shield,
  Nor question the errand on which I go.

VI.

"I'll seek the besieger in his camp,
  And hither will haste with his reply:
Thine honor, be sure, is well secure
  With her who would live for thee, or die."

VII.

The Count looked up with a vacant air,
  As the slow nay rose to his lips so wan;
And he flung his arm as to clasp from harm
  The tender pleader, but — she was gone.

VIII.

And, ere he could order his wildered thought,
  The postern opened and closed again;
And he saw, in affright, with a pennon white,
  His Chrimhilde glide o'er the tented plain.

IX.

"By the pity of God, your grace!" she cried,
  And on unchallenged her way she went,
All weak as she was, till her step had pause
  In front of the startled chieftain's tent.

X.

As the sunset glinted her golden hair
  And her blue eyes lifted to intercede,
To the soldier it seemed as if he dreamed
  That the Mother of Christ had come to plead.

XI.

And stately she stood as stands a queen
  Who sovranly makes her mandates known:
"I have come to yield this dinted shield,
  Sir Baron, if thou the terms wilt own.

XII.

"Count Conrad's castle shall hence be thine,
If out of the garrison's chosen men,
Who have nobly fought as the noblest ought,
Thou passest in freedom, only ten.

XIII.

"Count Conrad's riches shall fill thine hands,
If forth thou grantest me leave to take
Some treasures I hold priced over gold:
Now promise it, for thy knighthood's sake!"

XIV.

The Baron all dazed by her royal mien,
And awed by her beauty, nothing loth
To answer a prayer so seeming fair,
Swore on the battered shield his oath.

XV.

"And now, my treasures — they are but twain,
Husband and child — thou grantest so?"
She paused: for reply, in the Baron's eye
There sparkled a tear, as he bade her go.

THE ROYALLEST GIFT.

Long centuries since, in the Rhine-land,
  There reigned a valorous king,
Who, out of his war-won treasures,
  Vowed unto the Lord to bring

Some token of fair requital:
  "A fane," he said, "that shall seem,
In its marvel of stone-work frostings,
  Like the cunningest craftsman's dream.

"I'll lavish my vast abundance
  With open, unreck'ning hand;
And still be the richest monarch
  That rules in this Western land.

"Albeit from base to roof-cope,
  My grandeur shall mark the whole,
There still is the unseen rubble
  My vassals have leave to dole.

"Then hearken and heed, good people!
  Bring hither your tithings all,
For I will reject no pittance
  Ye offer, howe'er so small."

Thereafter the work went forward
  Right nobly; and each did bring
Out of their meagre hoardings
  Some slenderest offering.

As the statued walls rose skyward,
  And blossoms bloomed out from stone,
It chanced that a rude-clad woman,
  As she watched, one day, made moan:

"If one of these workers love Thee,
  As I, — Thou Lord, dost know;
And yet I am empty-handed
  Of witness to prove it so.

"Even yonder the straining oxen,
  That drag at the heavy beam,
Are toiling in Thy sweet service:
  How spent with their work they seem!

"Dear Lord, since for *Thee* they labor,
  Hard-wrought on the king's high-way,
What hinders that I should give them
  The corn I have gleaned to-day?"

—When grand in its towered glory,
  The beautiful minster shone,
The eyes of the wondering people
  Saw graved on a mystic stone,

The name of the royallest giver
  Whose largess had crowned the fane:
Behold! 'twas an unknown woman's,
  And they searched for the king's in vain.

THE LADY RIBERTA'S HARVEST.

I.

In the days of eld there was wont to be,
On the jagged coast of the Zuyder Zee,
A city from whence broad galleons went
To distant island and continent,
To lands that under the tropics lay,
Ind and the fabled far Cathay,
To gather from earth, and sea, and air,
All that was beautiful, rich, and rare.
And back they voyaged so laden full
With fairy fabrics from old Stamboul;
With pungent woods that breathed out balms;
With broidered stuffs from the realm of palms;
With shawls from the marts of Ispahan;
With marvellous lacquers from strange Japan:
That through this traffic on many a sea,
So grand did its merchants grow to be,
That even Venetian lords became
Half covetous of the city's fame.

II.

The Lady Riberta's fleet was great,
  And year by year it had brought such store
Of treasures, until in her queenly state
  There scarcely sufficed her room for more.
Her feasts — no prince in the realms around
  Had service so rich or food so fine,
As daily her carven tables crowned;
  And proud she was of her luscious cates,
And her rare conserves, and her priceless wine,
  And her golden salvers and golden plates:
For all that the sea or the shore could bring,
Was hers for the fairest furnishing.

III.

It fell one day, that a stranger came
  In garb of an Eastern sage arrayed,
Commended by one of noble name:
  He had traversed many a clime, he said,
And, whithersoever he went, had heard
  Of the Lady Riberta's state, that so
In his heart a secret yearning stirred
  To find if the tale were true or no.

At once the Lady Riberta's pride
  Upsprang, and into her lordly hall
She led the stranger, and at her side
  She bade him be seated in sight of all.

IV.

Silver and gold around him gleamed,
The daintiest dishes before him steamed;
The rarest of fish, and flesh, and bird,
Fruits all flushed with the tropic sun,
Nuts whose names he had never heard,
Were offered: the stranger would have none;
Nor spake he in praise a single word.
"Doth any thing lack?" with chafe, at last,
The hostess queried, "from the repast?"
Gravely the guest then gave reply:
"Lady, since thou dost question, I,
Daring to speak the truth alway,
Even in such a presence, say
Something *is* wanting: I have sate
Oft at the tables of rich and great,
Nor seen such viands as these: but yet,
I marvel me much thou should'st forget
The world's one *best* thing: for 'tis clear,
Whatever beside, *it* is not here."

V.

"Name it," the Lady flashed, "and nought
Will I grudge of search till the *best* is brought."
But never another word the guest
Uttered, as soothly he waived aside
Her question, that in the heat of pride,
Mindless of courtesy, still she pressed.
And when from her grand refection hall
They fared from their feasting, one and all,
Again with a heightened tone and air
To the guest she turned, but no guest was there.
"I'll have it," she stamped, "whatever it be;
I'll scour the land, and I'll sweep the sea,
Nor ever the tireless quest resign
Till I know the world's one *best* thing mine!"

VI.

Once more were the white-sailed galleons sent
To far-off island and continent,
In search of the most delicious things
That ever had whetted the greed of kings:
But none of the luxuries that they brought,
Seemed quite the marvel the Lady sought.

VII.

At length from his latest voyage back
  Sailed one of her captains : he told her how
Wild weather had driven him from his track,
  And his vessel had sprung aleak, till bow
And stern were merged, and a rime of mould
Had mossed the flour within the hold,
And nothing was left but wine and meat,
Through weary weeks, for the crew to eat.
"Then the words of the stranger rose," he said,
"And I felt that the one *best* thing was *bread:*
And so, for a cargo, I was fain
Thereafter to load my ships with grain."

VIII.

The Lady Riberta's wrath out-sprang
Like a sword from its sheath, and her keen voice rang
Sharp as a lance-thrust: "Get thee back
To the vessels, and have forth every sack,
And spill in the sea thy cursèd store,
Nor ever sail with my galleons more!"

IX.

The people who hungered for daily bread,
Prayed that to them in their need, instead,
The grain might be dealt: but she heeded none,
Nor rested until the deed was done.

X.

The months passed on, and the harvest sown
In the furrows of deep sea-fields had grown
To a forest of slender stalks, — a wide
Strong net to trap whatever the tide
Drew on in its wake, — the drift and wreck
Of many a shattered mast and deck,
And all the tangle of weeds there be
Afloat in the trough of the plunging sea.
Until as the years went by, a shoal
Of sand had tided a sunken mole
Across the mouth of the port, that so
The galleys were foundered; and to and fro
No longer went forth: and merchants sought
Harbors elsewhere for the stores they brought.
The Lady Riberta's ships went down
In the offing: the city's old renown
Faded and fled with its commerce dead,
And the Lady Riberta *begged for bread.*

XI.

The hungry billows with rage and roar
Have broken the ancient barriers o'er,

And bitten their way into the shore,
And where such traffic was wont to be,
The voyager now can only see
The spume and fret of the Zuyder Zee.

HERIBERT'S KISS.

I.

"WHITHER away have sped huntsmen and knights and all,
While I have loitered here watching the waterfall?
Yonder the dark comes down over the Mummelsee;
What if its haunting sprites shower their spells on me?"

II.

And the page so debonair in scarlet and gold arrayed,
Rushed hither and yon to find the path to the open glade:
His bugle he loudly blew, and then as he paused to hear,
Only the dying fall of its echo swept his ear.

III.

"In the Black Forest — lost!" — but even the while he spake,
Keenly his searching eye turned to the misty lake,
And there, through the rifts of green, he saw on the lonely strand
A shallop, and from it sprang a youth on the beaching sand.

IV.

"God's benison!" Heribert cried: "the Duke and his
hunters chase
Out of my reach the boar home to his hiding-place
Deep in the hills, while I, musing with idle mind,
Only through silence learn how far I am left behind."

V.

Then, with a courteous air, guidance of him he sought,
But mutely the youth stalked on, as though he had
heard him not;
And Heribert followed close, till they reached a castle
door:
"What castle, forsooth?" he asked; but his guide was
seen no more.

VI.

He wound his bugle-horn, and a hoary seneschal
Lowered the creaking draw, and led him across the
hall:
He parted the arras' folds, and, out of the murk and
gloom,
Half wildered and blind he passed to the blaze of a
gorgeous room.

VII.

There on the däis sate a beautiful maiden, clad
In bridal snow: and yet her face had an aspect sad
As a nun's beneath her veil, and lower she dropped her
eye,
As Heribert told his tale, and waited for her reply.

VIII.

When with a gentle stress, he pleadingly begged a sign
Of grace, she calmly rose, and poured him a cup of wine.
He drank, and his senses swam, and his heart was
touched to flame,
As he gazed on the maiden's brow, and blushingly
sought her name.

IX.

" Erma of Windeck," slow, she answered; " of all
bereft,
I am the last lone stalk of a stately lineage left."
Heribert heard with joy, and, dropping upon his knee,
—" I will be more than all, all thou hast lost, to thee! "

X.

Quick from his finger he his mother's troth-ring drew,
And slid it upon the hand that whitely hung in view:

Instant a rapturous flash reddened her pallid brow:
"I have waited for this so long! Come to the chapel now."

XI.

And as they trode the aisle, a touch she lightly laid
On a sculptured statue there, in cassock and stole arrayed:
Out from its niche it stepped, and followed them slow and pale,
And solemnly stood with hands pressing the altar-rail.

XII.

"Heribert, Count of Klein, standest thou here to wed
Erma of Windeck now, — the living among the dead?"
Heribert's lips waxed white through passion and shock of bliss,
As he stooped to the virgin brow, and gave, for reply, a kiss.

XIII.

— Rumble and crash and start! What did he seem to hear?
Only his pawing steed, neighing beside his ear;
Only the far-off shout of the flying huntsman's glee,
Only the dreamy lap of the mystic Mummelsee.

FROM THE LIFE

OF

TO-DAY.

THE HERO OF THE COMMUNE.

I.

"GARÇON! You—*you*
Snared along with this cursèd crew?
(Only a child, and yet so bold,
Scarcely as much as ten years old!)
Do you hear? do you know
Why the *gensdarmes* put you there, in the row,
You, with those Commune wretches tall,
With your face to the wall?"

II.

"*Know?* To be sure I know! why not?
We're here to be shot;
And there, by the pillar, 's the very spot,
Fighting for France, my father fell:
Ah, well!—
That's just the way *I* would choose to fall,
With my *back* to the wall!"

III.

("Sacre! Fair, open fight, I say,
Is something right gallant in its way,
And fine for warming the blood; but who
Wants wolfish work like this to do?
Bah! 'tis a butcher's business!) *How?*
(The boy is beckoning to me now:
I knew that his poor child's heart would fail,
. . . . Yet his cheek's not pale:)
Quick! say your say, for don't you see,
When the Church-clock yonder tolls out *Three,*
You're all to be shot?
—*What?*
'*Excuse you one moment*'? O, ho, ho!
Do you think to fool a *gendarme* so?"

IV.

"But, sir, here's a watch that a friend, one day
(My father's friend), just over the way,
Lent me; and if you'll let me free,
—It still lacks seven minutes of *Three,*—
I'll come, on the word of a soldier's son,
Straight back into line, when my errand's done."

V.

"Ha, ha! No doubt of it! Off! Begone!
(Now, good Saint Dennis, speed him on!
The work will be easier since *he's* saved;
For I hardly see how I *could* have braved
The ardor of that innocent eye,
    As he stood and heard,
    While I gave the word,
Dooming him like a dog to die.")

VI.

"In time! Well, thanks, that my desire
Was granted; and now, I am ready:—Fire!
    One word!—that's all!
—You'll let me turn my *back* to the wall?"

VII.

"Parbleu! Come out of the line, I say,
Come out! (Who said that his name was *Ney*?)
Ha! France will hear of him yet one day!"

IN AN EASTERN BAZAAR.

I.

I AM tired! Let us sit in the shadow
  This mosque flings, and puff a cigar,
And watch, as they come from yon meadow,
  Those carriers, each with his jar:
  How lithe and how languid they are!

II.

Confess now, 'tis something delicious
  To leave the old life all behind,
Its turbulence, worries, and wishes,
  Its labors and longings, and find
  A Nirwâna, for once, to your mind.

III.

What softness suffuses the picture!
  How tranquil the poppied repose!
See the child there, unbound by the stricture
  Of dress that encumbers: *he* knows
  (All nude of the gyves we impose,)

IV.

What the meaning of *freedom* is better
  Than any young Frank of them all,
Whose civilized feet we must fetter,
  Whose white Christian limbs we must gall
  With garments that chafe and enthrall.

V.

Just look at yon brown caryatid
  Who poises the urn on her head;
Don't tell me her long locks are matted,
  But mark the Greek Naiad instead, —
  Such grace to such symmetry wed!

VI.

Quick! notice the droop of her shoulder,
  As she lowers the urn to her arm:
None ever will tell, or has told her
  How perfect she is: there's the charm!
  Such knowledge brings nothing but harm.

VII.

Here's a group now: The jealous Zenanas
  Unveil in the twilight their bowers;
And girls that look proud as Sultanas,
  Bloom out as the night-blooming flowers,
  That drowse, with their langours, the hours.

VIII.

True wildings of nature! Each gesture
  A study, by art undefiled;
They gather or loosen their vesture,
  By no thought of observance beguiled,
  Unconscious of aim as a child.

IX.

The traffic too:—What now could ruffle
  This white-turban'd Aryan's repose,
As, placidly scorning the scuffle
  And chaffer, he waits? for he knows
  Whose the vantage will be at the close.

X.

I miss, (and how restful the feeling!)
  As I catch the low hum of these hives,
That Occident worry that's stealing
  (Through schemes that our culture contrives,)
  The calmness all out of our lives.

XI.

No exigence harries their pleasures;
  Unbeautiful haste does not fray
Their time of its margin of leisures:
  While *we*, in our prodigal way,
  Forestall a whole morrow to-day.

XII.

Yes — yes — I concede we're their betters,
  Self-gratulant Goth that I am!
We have science, religion, and letters, —
  With the bane of the curse we've the balm:
  They keep their inviolate calm.

XIII.

If only this land of the lotus
  Would teach us the charm it knows best,
That could soothe the rasp'd nerve, — that could float us
  Far off to some Island of Rest,
  — What a boon from the East to the West!

ALPENGLOW.

I.

— YES, that's what I said;
The grass has been greening above his head
Two summers and more, yet — I scarce know why —
There was that in his smile that *could* not die,
For it *has* not died. In this autumn ray,
(Ah, me! the third since he went away!)
'Tis palpable as the Alpenglow
That clings to the footless slopes of snow,
As if to lighten, through evengloam,
Some loitering mountain-climber home;
Or rather, — turn to the sunset hills
Yonder, and mark how the shadow fills
All of their sadden'd faces: one, —
The amber'd peak that is next the sun,
Holds yet to its breast, as I to mine,
A glint of the still remembered shine:

— Well, that is the way
With the smile I was telling you of to-day.

II.

Have you watched a bird
Ever poise itself when something stirred
Its spirit to song? A quiver of throat,
The croon of a tremulous, trial note,
The catch with a crowding rapture crowned,
Then, — floods, where the swooning soul was drowned!
Even so, I have often sat apart
And marked the flutter about his heart
Thrill to his lips, as with a hum
Of voiceless music it seemed to come
And ripple around his mouth, with shy,
Impassionate answers of the eye,
While an overflush of marvellous grace
Would master, a-sudden, all his face,
Till the delicate nostril curved and swelled,
And the glance an eloquent sparkle held,
And a sense of song would come and go,
Such as dreamers watched by Ariel, know:
— Well, that was the way
With the smile I was telling you of to-day.

III.

And because I said
The grass has been greening above his head
Two summers and o'er, shall I think, therefore,
That smile can never be kindled more?
— That the grave could hold it, that cannot hold
Captive one straggling gleam of gold?
— That it's prisoned away in ashen'd clay,
As centuried sunbeams are to-day
'Neath fathoms of blacken'd strata? No!
Can essence immortal perish so?
When clouds have gathered betwixt the star
And the vision that watches it blazing far
In limitless æther, shall the eye
Drop earthward, and lips that are faithless, sigh,
— "Ah me! for the mist, the murk, the rain!
I never shall find my star again:"
While, to spirits that come and go, its shine
Has never before seemed so divine?
— Well, that is the way
With the smile I was telling you of to-day.

ROSSEL.

I.

O WRECK of all chivalries! whither
  Has vanished thy glory? O France!
Shall the last of thy *fleurs-de-lis* wither
  Which the Uhlan has spared? Shall *his* lance
Be dropped with a gesture of pity?
  Shall the bomb-shell in harmlessness burst?
Shall the shot that has furrowed the city
  (Forbearing to compass the worst,)
Unscathed leave the best of your foemen,
  While ye, in your cowardice fell,
(Scared rulers) shoot down the one Roman
      Among them, — Rossel?

II.

"*A Communist?*" Ay, whose one crime was
  Too fervid a faith in his cause;
Too noble a trust that the time was
  The chosen of Fate, and a pause

Might rivet, for ages, the fetter
  That Liberty, crazed through despair,
Had rent in her frenziedness. "Better
  Die *then*, in their fury, and *there*,
Than yet by new masters be goaded!"
  — Success has its laurels, as well
As Failure its chains. . . . They have loaded
    The "felon" Rossel.

III.

Ah, short-sighted zealots of Order!
  Has mastery stricken you blind?
Was death the sole, pitiless warder
  Whose cell had no postern behind?
. . . The spirit whose ardor had fired
  A cause that was desperate — yea,
A Breton as brave as a Bayard,
  Could never have stooped to betray!
But Time shall avenge him: each lowland,
  Hill, plain, with his story shall swell,
As they say: *The Gironde had its Roland;*
    The Commune, Rossel!

HIS NAME.

(AN INCIDENT OF THE GREAT BOSTON FIRE.)

I.

O, THE billows of fire!
With maelstrom-like swirl,
Their surges they hurl
Over roof, over spire,
Mad, masterless, higher,
Till rumble — crack — crash —
Down boom with a flash,
Whole columns of granite and marble: see! see!
Sucked in as a weed on the ocean might be,
Or engulfed as a sail
In the hurricane-riot and wreak of the gale!

II.

Ha! yonder they rush where the death-dealing *steam*,
Over-pent, waits their gleam
To shudder the city with earthquake! Who, *who*
Will adventure mid-flame, and unfasten the screw,

Set the fiend loose, and save us so? Fireman, you —
You willing? Would God you might hazard it! Nay,
The red tongues are licking the faucets now! Stay!
Too late! — 'tis too late!
If ruin, explosion, *must* come, let us wait
Its coming: To go is to perish: — Hold! hold!
You are young — I am old —
You've a wife too, — and children? . . . O God! he is gone
Straight into destruction! The pipes, men! On — on!
Play the water-stream on him — full — faster — the whole!
And now . . . Christ save his soul!

III.

I stifle — I choke —
And *he* — Heaven grant that he smother in smoke
Ere the dread detonation! Hark — hark! What's the shout?
Is he saved? Is he out?
Did he compass his purpose? . . . The hero! *One* name
This pencil of fire on the records of Fame
Shall blazon, if justice is meted. Why here
On my cheek is a tear,
Which not a whole city in ashes could claim!
— His name, now, — *Can nobody tell me his name?*

A SOLILOQUY IN THE VATICAN.

(1873.)

WHAT ails the world? Can those last days be nearing,
  Foredoomed in the divine Apocalypse?
Of heresies my ears are stunned with hearing,
  Uncatholic schism our ancient empire strips
  Of half its power, and half is in eclipse.

O for the might St. Gregory's arm once wielded!
  (*In pace requiescat!*) Kaisers pay
No homage such as royal Henry yielded;*
  And my dead son of France, I loathly say,
  Proved but a poor St. Louis in his day.

In place of a Matilda,† bringing purely,
  With woman's grace, all aids to soothe my pain,
I smile upon (I own, somewhat demurely!)
  Her scarce immaculate Majesty of Spain:
  Ah! who will wear my *Golden Rose* again?

* Henry II., Emperor of Germany.

† Countess of Tuscany.

Yet none hath held, since Pontifex St. Peter
Here sate, so long as I, the sacred chair:
And when had Mother-Church such hosts to greet her
"Commemoration" past, as met to share
From every clime, her pomps and splendors rare?

Fixt is the tenet battled for through ages;
Infallible, henceforth, the Holy See;
And that illustrious dogma that engages
Ave Maria's saintly purity,
Both won: yet whence the gain of all — to *me?*

Has Heaven become ungrateful? Blessèd warder,
Who holdest in thy hand the mystic keys,
Hast thou no care for this unchecked disorder,
Content in Paradise to take thine ease?
Bethink thee — Thou once felt the surge of seas!

Cloistered in peace so long, hast thou no pity?
No prison-memories of thy Mamertine?
It *must* be! Else, in my Eternal City
Would I sit captive, questioning, "Is it mine?"
While Lombards fill once more the Esquiline; —

While radical railways, levelling schools, free Bibles,
Like the Campagna's breath, are poisoning Rome;

While printed sheets that spread infectious libels
  Are read (Heaven help!) beneath St. Peter's dome;
  While here another Alaric finds his home!

"Son of the Church," yet grudge the Holy Father
  His poor *polenta!* Never shall *he* kiss
This ruby on my finger here: far rather
  Forego such cozening fealty, and miss
  Henceforth that traitorous, "Master, hail!" of his!

Bismarck and Döllinger! The same sad story!
  Without, within, feigned friends and crafty foes:
Where will it end? I'll summon Monsignorè
  Good Antonelli; for he ever knows
  How best to balsam my despairs and woes.

O for the old, untroubled days of quiet,
  When loungers basked beside the fountains cool,
Unplagued by all this 'liberal' rant and riot,
  So they were fed, not caring who might rule:
  But now! — *The beggars vote and go to school!*

UNAWARES.

I.

We've passed each other in the street
  For years, my hem your garment sweeping;
And when we met in converse sweet,
Always the hours on silver feet
  Danced to the time your talk was keeping.

II.

I thought I knew you, heart and mind,
  Content o'er surface forms to linger;
Nor ever dreamed that what I've pined
And searched for all my life to find,
  Was just beneath my heedless finger.

III.

O, happy random touch and tone,
  Informed with sense beyond my seeing,
That to my inner eye has thrown
Open your guarded soul, and shown
  The latent treasures of your being!

IV.

Here is a cabinet: Over-seas
  It came, while yet Sir Walter's glory
Flung round his Virgin Colonies
The lustre of those chivalries
  That blazon all our earlier story.

V.

Some old Venetian wrought his life
  Into its countless, quaint vagaries:
Its ebon front with hints is rife,
Of all that moved him — children, wife, —
  A Satyr's face, and then a Mary's.

VI.

Early I learned each secret cell;
  Its sinuous maze I could unravel,
And held the clew, and knew the spell
Of every covert spring as well
  As windings of the garden-gravel.

VII.

But toying in an aimless way
  Some dusty, cobwebbed spaces under,
It chanced that I should touch one day
A spray of carvings, — when the spray
  Flew back, and left me mute with wonder.

VIII.

For there, to my astonished sight,
  Within a mouldy nook lay gleaming,
Beneath the sun's intrusive light,
An urn of carven malachite, —
  A cameo cut beyond my dreaming!

IX.

— To think what countless hood-winked eyes,
  Unconscious of the riches hidden
In reach, for ever missed the prize,
Which yet a touch so randomwise
  As mine, revealed to me unbidden!

X.

Here at my throat the gem I wear,
  O'er which my fancy loves to wander,
Deeming I trace Cellini there;
And see my other pride, — that rare
  Antique upon the bracket yonder.

INASMUCH.

THE day, with all its fervid hours
  Of golden possibility,
  Went down behind the sapphire sea;
And that dull sense of squandered powers,
Before whose waste the conscience cowers,
  Was all those hours had left to me.

Remorsefully I bowed my head
  And sighed: "Ah, Lord, Thy heart doth know
  I would not have the record so
Written above the day that's dead, —
Its doing and undoing done: Instead,
  My love had fanned a zeal whose glow

"Waited my touch to leap to flame;
  I felt the inbreathed power to write
  Words that Thy Spirit should indite;
And when I named Thy sacred Name,
The cloven inspiration came,
    As with a pentecostal might.

"I had no other thought to sing
Than for Thy glory: since I knew
No bird went breasting up the blue,
With throb of throat and strain of wing,
That did not in its measure bring
Accepted service, pure and true.

"That rapture past, I planned a deed
Of costly effort for Thy sake,
In which I charged that Self should take
No slightest share, nor flesh have heed,
Nor shrinking Will have let to plead,
Nor heart betray a conscious ache.

"And now the day within whose scope
I set my deeds, is dead and done,
And all my aims are missed: Not one
Of those with which I thought to cope
In dauntlessness of faith and hope,
Has ev'n so much as been begun."

As thus I moaned my self-complaint,
Across the midnight seemed to loom
A vision, and athwart the gloom

A whisper fell, so sweet, so faint,
That I looked up with strange constraint,
And lo! a brightness swam the room.

I sank o'erawed; and as I lay
With downward face, a dream of voice
Drifted above: it said, "Rejoice!
Thy dead day, wept for, lives, — a day
Vital with action, though it may
Have brought but failure to thy choice.

"Thy work undone, I take as though
Wrought to completion; and the strain
That throbs, unsung, within thy brain,
I hear in all its overflow,
And know as thou canst never know,
The silent music born of pain.

"'Twas *I* who bade the hindrance stir
Thy soul from singing, — *I* who laid
My hand upon thy hands, and stayed
Their chosen purpose, while to her
Who suffered, as a minister
I sent thee, erranding mine aid.

" And inasmuch as thou hast brought
  Thy draught of water, deemed so small ;
  And inasmuch as at My call
Thou didst the work thou hadst not sought,—
As double deeds, wrought and unwrought,
  I, needing none, accept them all."

ONE DAY.

A SONNET.

WHAT saith the sightless poet, brighter-eyed
  Through inward vision than all the bards of old?
  —The gods in wisdom, boundless, manifold,
Have reason's guidance unto men supplied,
Enough for one day's usage, — nought beside;
  And One to whom a thousand years are told
  Even as a tale, doth bid us have and hold
The day sufficient, — let whatso betide.

There *is* no morrow: Though before our face
  The shadow named so stretches, we alway
  Fail to o'ertake it, hasten as we may:
God only gives one island-inch of space
Betwixt the Eternities, as standing-place,
  Where each may work, — th' inexorable To-day!

SMITTEN.

A SONNET.

If I might only enter to thy soul
  And give thee comfort! But it were as though
  The stalwart oak, root-shaken by the blow
Of battling elements that rage and roll
With thunder-crash against the mighty bole,
  Should heed (while limbs are snapped, and to and fro,
  Its leafy robe, rent in access of woe,
Floats tempest-tossed), if faintly upward stole
The violet's whisper: "I, mid swirls that choke
  My sunshine out, with drowning eyes entreat
  That I may bear some fragrance, soothing-sweet,
In my small cup, to medicine the stroke
That strips and maims thee!"
                                        Ah, my ravaged oak,
  See! I am but the violet at thy feet!

DEAD DAYS.

I.

OUR summers are but burial-places where
We lay to rest the sweet days as they die,
Softening their outline with love's rosemary,
And memory's lavender, and all of rare
Tokens to keep them fair.

II.

Our winters are the vaults, whose ice-fring'd cells
Shut in our sorrow-shrouded days, for whom,
When borne and left amid their frozen gloom,
White-surplic'd flakes (in place of lily-bells)
Tinkle their muffled knells.

III.

We bury them, and sigh with bowing head,
Submissive else: The tender days *must* go,
For they are earthly-born, and perish so;
Yet by what augury hath any said
That they are *wholly* dead?

IV.

The short child-meted grave o'er which we yearn
  Even yet ; the empty bird's-nest filled with snows ;
  The leafless bough ; the Spring that comes and goes,
Teach resurrection lessons, each in turn,
          Which we are quick to learn.

V.

Our days die thus : and we, — their lives withdrawn, —
  Like other mourners, fail of faith's control,
  Forgetful that each memory is the soul
Of a dead day, such as in summers gone
          Midst rosemary sleeps on.

VI.

And when they meet us yonder, face to face,
  In the grand Easter-Morning — shall we then
  Hail them with greet and welcome once again,
Companions of our blessedness always,
          Dear, risen, deathless days ?

THE QUESTION.

A SONNET.

O Nature, gracious mother of us all,
Within thy bosom myriad secrets lie
Which thou surrenderest to the patient eye
That seeks and waits. But to the yearning call,
That has not ceased from hungering lips to fall
Reiterate, through the centuries sweeping by,
Thou hast not once vouchsafed assured reply,
Nor answered even with voicings still and small,
These eager questionings; — *Whence do we come?*
From what nonentity, to live our day?
And when this marvellous being melts away,
Whitherward do we go? To this, the sum
Of human mysteries, what hast thou to say?
Nought: Memnon-like, thy mighty lips are dumb.

GONE FORWARD.

I.

YES, "Let the tent be struck:" Victorious morning
  Through every crevice flashes in a day
Magnificent beyond all earth's adorning:
  The night is over; wherefore should he stay?
  And wherefore should our voices choke to say,
      "The General has gone forward"?

II.

Life's foughten field not once beheld surrender;
  But with superb endurance, present, past,
Our pure Commander, lofty, simple, tender,
  Through good, through ill, held his high purpose fast,
  Wearing his armor spotless, — till at last,
      Death gave the final, "*Forward.*"

III.

All hearts grew sudden palsied: Yet what said he
  Thus summoned? — "*Let the tent be struck!*" — For when
Did call of duty fail to find him ready

Nobly to do his work in sight of men,
For God's and for his country's sake — and then,
To watch, wait, or go forward?

IV.

We will not weep, — we dare not! Such a story
As his large life writes on the century's years,
Should crowd our bosoms with a flush of glory,
That manhood's type, supremest that appears
To-day, *he* shows the ages. Nay, no tears
Because he has gone forward!

V.

Gone forward? — Whither? — Where the marshall'd legions,
Christ's well-worn soldiers, from their conflicts cease; —
Where Faith's true Red-Cross knights repose in regions
Thick-studded with the calm, white tents of peace, —
Thither, right joyful to accept release,
The General has gone forward!

THE SHADE OF THE TREES.

WHAT are the thoughts that are stirring his breast?
  What is the mystical vision he sees?
— "*Let us pass over the river and rest*
    Under the shade of the trees."

Has he grown sick of his toils and his tasks?
  Sighs the worn spirit for respite or ease?
Is it a moment's cool halt that he asks
    Under the shade of the trees?

Is it the gurgle of waters whose flow
  Oft-time has come to him, borne on the breeze,
Memory listens to, lapsing so low,
    Under the shade of the trees?

Nay — though the rasp of the flesh was so sore,
  Faith that had yearnings far keener than these,
Saw the soft sheen of the Thitherward Shore,
    Under the shade of the trees; —

Caught the high psalms of ecstatic delight, —
  Heard the harps harping, like soundings of seas, —
Watched earth's assoilèd ones walking in white
    Under the shade of the trees.

O, was it strange he should pine for release,
  Touched to the soul with such transports as these, —
He who so needed the balsam of peace,
    Under the shade of the trees?

Yea, it was noblest for *him* — it was best,
  (Questioning naught of our Father's decrees,)
There to pass over the river and rest
    Under the shade of the trees!

AGASSIZ.

NOT to his native Pays de Vaud,
  Fringed with its Alpine glaciers wan,
Not to the pathless peaks whose snow
  Dazzled his childhood, has he gone.

Not to the goatherd's gloaming call
  Turned he to listen, ringing clear;
Not to the "kine-row" chant, of all
  Strains, most sweet to the Switzer's ear.

Tender the voice was, nor in vain
  Ever to him its least behest;
—"Tired out spirit, wearied brain,
  Into my quiet come and rest."

Even as once our Poet said,*
  Long had he traversed ways untrod,
Finding in signs none else had read,
  Many a hieroglyph of God.

* Mr. Longfellow's Birthday poem.

Meekly from Nature's lips he learned,
  Tracking her steps from shore to shore,
Secrets o'er which his soul had yearned, —
  Marvels she never had told before.

How at her hints, his heart would stir,
  Still on her shy suggestions bent,
Whether through seas he followed her,
  Whether o'er breadths of continent!

Toilers for self might take the fame
  Waiting to crown their toilings so:
Careless of ease, or wealth, or name,
  All that *he* asked was, — leave to *know*.

So, as he bowed with lowly head,
  Patiently conning the tasks she set,
Softly the Teacher stooped and said,
  — "Now, that thou knowest thine alphabet, —

"Come from this narrow cosmic rule
  Straitened through ignorance, blight and curse,
Home to thy Father's grander school,
  Into His boundless universe!"

SANDRINGHAM.

I.

Even here, within Sir Walter's Old Dominion,
Among Virginian valleys shut away,
Meeting, we questioned of the last opinion, —
"What tidings come from Sandringham to-day?"

II.

Midst the wild rush of our tumultuous cities,
Whose billowy tides plunge seething on their way,
The throb that stirred all hearts, was inmost pity's —
"Hope scarcely breathes at Sandringham to-day."

III.

Along the ice-chained waters of Saint Lawrence,
From fur-wrapt sledge, — on crowded street and quay, —
A flood of eager askings poured their torrents,
— "What latest word from Sandringham to-day?"

IV.

On the lone out-posts of our Southern borders,
Where watch-fires keep the scalping-knife at bay,
There mingled strangely with the morning "orders,"
The call, — "Some news from Sandringham to-day?"

V.

Where sits the golden Queen of the Pacific,
Glad wives with broken voices, paused to say,
—"*Sweet Princess!*" (while their brows grew beatific,)
—"God bless her!—*hope* at Sandringham to-day!"

VI.

Out o'er the Occident's wide reach of ocean,
Wherever vessels crossed each others' way,
The trumpet blared abroad the strong emotion,
—"Hoy!—Life or death at Sandringham to-day?"

VII.

From Hoogly's Mouth to Kyber-Pass went flashing
The quick inquiry: Where Australia's spray
Closed o'er dropt anchors, through the breakers dashing,
Sailors cried—"What of Sandringham to-day?"

VIII.

The diamond delver, reeking under torrid
Colonial suns that poured their blinding ray,
Sighed as he raised to heaven his burning forehead,
—"Spare, Lord, the life at Sandringham to-day!"

IX.

The same sweet yearning of responsive pity
Went up all whither Christian people pray;
And Continental city asked of city,
"What bulletin from Sandringham to-day?"

X.

In every English home, — by Scottish ingle, —
At Ireland's hearths; — on lone Welsh mountains gray,
All hearts now with the girdling gladness tingle,
— "There's life, — hope, — health, at Sandringham to-day!"

XI.

— *Is faith lost in the human?* — Are ye able,
Cold cynics, in your scorn, to rend away
The marvellous strands of that electric cable
That links the world with Sandringham to-day? [10]

THROUGH THE PASS.

(Matthew F. Maury's last Wish.)

I.

"Home, — bear me home, at last," — he said,
"And lay me where my dead are lying,
But not while skies are overspread,
And mournful wintry winds are sighing.

II.

"Wait till the royal march of Spring
Carpets your mountain fastness over, —
Till chattering birds are on the wing,
And buzzing bees are in the clover.

III.

"Wait till the laurel bursts its buds,
And creeping ivy flings its graces
About the lichen'd rocks, and floods
Of sunshine fill the shady places.

IV.

"Then, when the sky, the air, the grass,
Sweet Nature all, is glad and tender,
Then bear me through 'The Goshen Pass'
Amid its flush of May-day splendor."

V.

— So *will* we bear him! Human heart
To the warm Earth's drew never nearer,
And never stooped she to impart
Lessons to one who held them dearer.

VI.

Stars lit new pages for him: seas
Revealed the depths their waves were screening;
The ebbs gave up their masteries,
The tidal flows confessed their meaning.

VII.

Of ocean-paths, the tangled clew
He taught the nations to unravel;
And mapped the track where safely through
The lightning-footed thought might travel.

VIII.

And yet, unflattered by the store
  Of these supremer revelations,
Who bowed more reverently before
  The lowliest of earth's fair creations?

IX.

What sage of all the sages past
  Ambered in Plutarch's limpid story,
Upon the age he served, has cast
  A radiance touched with worthier glory?

X.

His noble living for the ends
  God set him, — (duty underlying
Each thought, word, action,) — naught transcends
  In lustre, save his nobler dying.

XI.

— Do homage, sky, and air, and grass,
  All things he cherished, sweet and tender,
As through our gorgeous mountain-pass
  We bear him in the May-day splendor!

KINGSLEY.

(JANUARY 24TH, 1875.)

ONE voice the less to plead with men
  For God's down-trodden poor;
One hand the less to wield the pen
  With aim so bold and sure;
One heart the less to pity, when
  The ill was past his cure!

Through Britain's length of island strand—
  From bald Ben Lomond's head
To Devon's reach of silver sand—
  The sudden tidings spread;
And there was shadow on the land,
  Because this man was dead.

How had that active brain been stressed,
  That tender heart been wrung!

What eloquence had poured its zest
Through that persuasive tongue,
That hoary wrongs might be redressed,
And Work's true idyl sung!

With life scarce past its equinox,
Its shortening days still fair,
We stagger at the blow that mocks
The deeds he yet might dare.
— Who now will bid the "Alton Lockes"
Rise from their grim despair?

What arm will fling the banner high
On which the legend ran:
"*Room in the lists to fight or die!*
— Let conquer him who can!"
What lips take up his tilting-cry:
"The Brotherhood of Man?"

Full fairly has he won his prize,
A prize the proud may scorn —
That thousand honest English eyes,
Once hopeless and forlorn,
To-day lift brighter to the skies,
Because this man was born.

Too busied with his ends to weigh
  The charm or cheat of fame,
While routed wrong maintained the fray—
  Unsought the guerdon came;
—The wires that coil the world to-day
  All vibrate with his name!

SONNETS.

BLEMISHED OFFERING.

I.

"I WOULD my gift were worthier!" — sighed the
Greek,
As on he goaded to the temple-door
His spotted bullock. "Ever of our store
Doth Zeus require the best; and fat and sleek
The ox I vowed to him — (no brindled streak,
No fleck of dun,) when through the breakers' roar
He bore me safe, that day, to Naxos' shore;
And now, — my gratitude, — how seeming-weak!

"But here be chalk-pits: What if I should white
The blotches, hiding all unfitness so?
The victim in the people's eyes would show
Better therefor; — the sacrificial rite
Be quicklier granted at thus fair a sight,
And the great Zeus himself might never know."

II.

We have a God who *knows:* And yet we dare
On His consuming altar-coals to lay
(Driven by the prick of conscience to obey)
The whited sacrifice, the hollow prayer,
In place of what we vowed, in our despair,
Of best and holiest; — glad no mortal may
Pierce through the cheat, and hoping half to stay
That Eye before whose search all souls are bare!

Nay rather; — Let us bring the victim-heart
Defiled, unworthy, blemished, though it be,
And fling it on the flame, entreating, — "See —
I blush to know how vile in every part
Is this my gift, through sin's delusive art,
Yet, 'tis the best that I can offer Thee!"

BECAUSE.

(J. R. T.)

THIS friend now, — a month or so only
  Ago, and you smiled in his smile ;
And when he grew weary or lonely,
  You jested, to cheer him the while :
He prized the sweet solace you proffered,
  For gloom giving laughter instead :
— You are glad of the gift that you offered,
      Because, — *he is dead.*

And *because* he is dead, shall we gather
  The humanest relics there be,
(All tenderer, dearer, the rather !)
  And pile up a Pagan suttee ?
Shall we speak of him, brows bending lowly ?
  Shall we whisper his name underbreath ?
— Is not life in its living as holy
      And solemn as death ?

As death? — What *is* death but the ending
  Of all that the mortal can claim?
— The drop of the mantle descending
  From the soul's mounting chariot of flame!
Who pitied the prophet when guerdon
  So grand was requiting all loss?
— Weep for *him* left behind, — with the Jordan
      Of trial to cross!

Ah, surely the angels who love us,
  Must yearn with an ache of desire
To show us, — poor blindlings! — above us,
  The pathway still trailed with the fire; —
Must melt with compassion to urge us,
  As, shuddering, we shrink from the tide,
To smite, till the faith-smitten surges
      Of doubt shall divide.

So, — speak of our friend who is walking
  In his chorister-garments of white,
With the calm that would mellow your talking,
  If he sat in your presence to-night:

Yea,—name him with gladder elation,
  With fonder contentment, and shred
No brightness from out the narration,
    Because he is dead!

To M. B. D.

MYRRH-BEARERS.

(IN ANCIENT GREEK ART THE MARYS WERE CALLED,—
"MYROPHORES.")

THREE women crept at break of day
A-grope along the shadowy way,
Where Joseph's tomb and garden lay.

With blanch of woe each face was white,
As the gray Orient's waxing light
Brought back upon their awe-struck sight

The sixth-day scene of anguish: Fast
The starkly-standing cross they passed,
And, breathless, neared the gate at last.

Each on her throbbing bosom bore
A burden of such fragrant store
As never there had lain before.

Spices the purest, richest, best,
That e'er the musky East possessed,
From Ind to Araby-the-Blest,

Had they with sorrow-riven hearts,
Searched all Jerusalem's costliest marts
In quest of; — nards whose pungent arts

Should the dead sepulchre imbue
With vital odors through and through:
— 'Twas all their love had leave to do!

Christ did not need their gifts: — And yet
Did either Mary once regret
Her offering? — Did Salomé fret

Over the unused aloes? — Nay!
They counted not as waste, that day,
What they had brought their Lord: — The way

Home, seemed the path to Heaven: They bare,
Thenceforth, about the robes they ware,
The clinging perfume everywhere.

— So, ministering as erst did these,
Go women forth by twos and threes,
(Unmindful of their morning ease,)

Through tragic darkness, murk and dim,
Where'er they see the faintest rim
Of promise, — all for sake of Him

Who rose from Joseph's tomb. They hold
It just such joy as those of old,
To tell the tale the Marys told.

Myrrh-Bearers still, — at home, abroad,
What paths have holy women trod,
Burdened with votive gifts for God, —

Rare gifts, whose chiefest worth was priced
By this one thought, that all sufficed;
— *Their spices had been bruised for Christ!*

BY-AND-BY.

WHAT will it matter by-and-by,
  Whether my path below was bright,
  Whether it wound through dark or light,
Under a gray or a golden sky,
When I look back on it, by-and-by?

What will it matter by-and-by,
  Whether, unhelped, I toiled alone,
  Dashing my foot against a stone,
Missing the charge of the angel nigh,
Bidding me think of the by-and-by?

What will it matter by-and-by,
  Whether with dancing Joy I went
  Down through the years with a gay content,
Never believing, — nay, not I,
Tears would be sweeter by-and-by!

What will it matter by-and-by,
  Whether with cheek to cheek I've lain
  Close by the pallid angel, Pain,

Soothing myself through sob and sigh,
—"All will be elsewise, by-and-by!"

What will it matter?—Naught, if I
  Only am sure the way I've trod,
  Gloomy or gladdened, leads to God,
Questioning not of the how, the why,
If I but reach Him, by-and-by.

What will I care for the unshared sigh,
  If, in my fear of lapse or fall,
  Close I have clung to Christ through all,
Mindless how rough the road might lie,
Sure He will smoothen it by-and-by.

What will it matter by-and-by?
  Nothing but this;—That Joy or Pain
Lifted me skyward,—helped to gain,
Whether through rack, or smile, or sigh,
Heaven,—Home,—All in All,—by-and-by!

AGNES.

I.

SURELY there hangs a dimmer shine
  Over the sky than a month ago;
Droppings of tears this soughing pine
  Holds in its voice,—it is sobbing so:
Yonder a lonely robin weaves
  Heart-breaks into his plaintive weet;
Even the scarlet maple-leaves
  Sink with a sigh about my feet;
And Indian-Summer's haze droops wan,
      —*Agnes has gone!*

II.

There is the reason: Out of the sky,
  Purpled and paled with dreamy mist,
Shaken from breezy wafts that lie
  Calmed in their isles of amethyst,
Gurgling from every bird that croons,
  Heard in the leaf-fall,—heard in the rain,

Under the nights, and under the noons, —
  Ever there sounds the sad refrain,
Throbbing and sobbing over and on,
  — "*Agnes has gone!*"

III.

Ah, can we live and bear to miss
  Out of our lives this life how rare?
— Tender, *so* tender! an angel's kiss
  Hallowed it daily, unaware:
Gracious as sunshine, sweet as dew
  Shut in a lily's golden core,
Fragrant with goodness through and through,
  Pure as the spikenard Mary bore;
Holy as twilight, soft as dawn,
  — Agnes has gone!

LETTING-GO OF HANDS.

I.

O, THE chill, clinging crush of the fingers,
  Each pressure more faint than the last!
O, the slackening hold that still lingers,
  Though the wrench of the spirit be past!
What heart, in its holpelessness breaking
  To feel them, can stifle the cry
The human within us is making,
  — "God help, — or we die!"

II.

We wring with a passion of sorrow,
  We cover with kisses of pain,
The palm that some fairer to-morrow,
  We'll fold in old fondness again.
. . . We drop the pale fingers, whose colding
  Impassiveness startles our own,
For ever — (how oft!) — from our holding,
  And yet not a moan

III.

Breaks from us : — The spirit is deadened
  To numbness because of the blow ;
We know that the sunshine has leadened,
  Has blackened ; 'tis all that we know :
We only can wonder, thus letting
  Hands go, that we keep, as we may,
(— As we *must*, —) life within us, — forgetting
    That grief does not slay.

IV.

Does not slay : — or how often, in lonely
  Despairs, would we hail it instead,
Of friends the most friendly, if only
  It let us lie down by our dead !
But with gall and with wormwood of anguish,
  Through silences stronger than tears,
It nerves us to bear, as we languish
    Along the gray years.

V.

And kind ones, in soothingest fashion,
  (Not always ev'n Love understands !)

Speak low in their yearning compassion,
  Of the beautiful folding of hands
Vouchsafed to the weary, — of graspings,
  For which the long-parted so pine:
— What comfort to *me* the keen claspings,
      When the clasp is not *mine!*

VI.

O hands that lie crossing so saintly
  The bosoms on which I have leant!
Could I press them, though ever so faintly,
  Just once, . . . I would wait with content
For the time that so loiters, so lingers,
  When, with rapture undreamed-of before,
I catch to my lips the dear fingers,
      And loose them no more!

PROPHETS OF DOUBT.

ONE lifts aloft his vatic cry,
  And bids the race believe in Man,
  The possible and perfect Pan,
Who, if he wills it, may defy
  Whate'er of evil shares control
  With good, in his warfaring soul,
And find his heaven beneath the sky.

One craves with more than Attic zest,
  The fair Greek calm all statue-wrought
  To Phidian fineness, — pleasures caught
From sensuous Nature at her best;
  Too lotos-lapped, Endymion-wise,
  To front with Eastern-gazing eyes
The jar and jostle of the West.

One meets us with a rolick air,
  And while he twirls his Ring and Book,
Propounds with serious-comic look,
  Some paradox: Yet points us where

She sings, — 'half angel and half bird,'
Whose faith no Delphic doubt has blurred
With fumes of a sublime despair.

One pacing slow beside the seas
That belt his island-home, can find
No voice to hush the questioning mind,
Or win the wrestling spirit ease;
No gleam upon 'the altar-stairs,'
No test assured, save his who bears
Beneath his cloak the jangled 'keys.'

One with a pale, pathetic gloom
About his brows, beats on his breast
And moans: — "I find no anchor'd rest
Safe from the surge of doubt or doom:
I pant to break the bars that prison
My bonded soul: *Christ is not risen!*
The seal is yet upon His tomb!"

One dreams above the gray-grown Past,
But with a brow so earthly-sad,
That even his May-tides scarce seem glad,
And ó'er his happiest skies are cast

A creeping chill, a curdling breath,
Like cerecloth on the face of Death,
Death that still ends the tale at last.

One a new Gospel would rehearse
In place of old dogmatic creed:
—Through Culture shall the mind be freed
From all of past or present curse;
Till by its Sweetness and its Light,
An out-grown God be banished quite
Beyond the self-caused universe.

And one, the last, his glowing lyre
Cooled with Arcadian violets, sings
Just what the veriest Pagan's strings
Gave forth, before Promethean fire
Into his leaping pulses stole,
And taught him how the royal soul
Disdains the senses' mean attire.

— O, Prophets of a younger day!
O, Seers of an unfaith that seems
To shift with every dreamer's dreams,
And veer with every meteor's ray, —

Can phosphorescent sparks like these
Guide thro' the trough of gulfing seas,
Wrecks drifting in despair away?

What help is here for hearts undone?
What stay for frantic souls? What hope
For piercing prayers that wildly grope
After the peace they have not won,
Across th' abysmal spaces? — Who
Implores not some diviner clew
To lead him to the central sun?

Keep then your sad negations, iced
With darkness, doubt, and frore despair;
Bind up your vision, and declare
That no Evangel has sufficed,
(Despite the faith of myriads dead,)
Upon your deviate paths to shed
The light ye seek: But leave *us* CHRIST!

THE GRANDEST DEED.

I.

The myriad messengers of God
  Before the central throne
Waited, — attent to fly abroad,
  And make His errands known
Wherever foot of man had trod,
  Or angel wing had flown.

Nor any asked, if great or small
  The task, his portioned share
A kingdom's or a sparrow's fall
  They held an equal care;
His work, the same, supreme in all,
  Who governs everywhere.

II.

One spirit to a world afar
  In utmost æther went;
And one to seek a new-born star,
  On mission vast intent;
And one, where circling systems are
  Uncatalogued, was sent.

Came one, — the mightiest: O'er his face
  He spread his veiling wing,
To soften the effulgent blaze
  Of God's forthshadowing,
And craved, that he to Heaven's high praise
  Some added joy might bring.

III.

To him the errand fell: — "Thou seest
  Where yonder spark doth shine
Beneath thee, — one among the least
  Of these fair worlds of Mine;
Yet honored even above the rest
  By gifts the most divine:

Go tell its dwellers how my Christ,
  Through human guise, made dim
The glory that in Heaven sufficed
  To dazzle cherubim;
And bid them, other faiths despised,
  Believe alone in *Him*."

I.

Again before the emerald throne
  The messengers of God
Stood flushed with tidings: They had gone
  Through worlds on worlds abroad,
Wherever angel wing had flown,
  Or foot of man had trod.

And one had triumphs strange to tell,
  By infinite Wisdom wrought;
And one had works ineffable,
  To grand achievement brought;
And one had mystic lore, to swell
  Seraphic bound of thought.

II.

—"Who hath believèd *thy* report?"—
  And at the questioning word,
Throughout the vast celestial court,
  Uplifting wings were heard,
As if some news of gladder sort
  Their crowding hosts had stirred.

And as the throb of silence sank
  Where loud the song had been,
They parted, seven-fold rank on rank,
  To let the angel in,
Who backward from the radiance shrank,
  Nor audience sought to win.

III.

Lowly he spake: — "Thy word I bore
  To men by sin enslaved;
And thousands heard it o'er and o'er,
  Nor grace, nor pardon craved:
Yet one who never heard before,
  One heathen soul was saved."

Then through the circling ranks serene,
  The joy that thrilled the whole,
Brake forth in rapture; while between,
  Ten thousand harpings stole:
— The grandest deed of all had been
  To save that heathen soul!

COMFORTED.

THERE are who tell me I should be
  So firm of faith, so void of fear,
  So buoyed by calm, courageous cheer,
(Assured, through Christ's security,
  There is a place prepared,) that I
  Should dare not be afraid to die.

They question of the nameless dread,
  With lifted brow, — as if I let
  Unreasoning foretastes overfret
My soul unduly, while I tread
  A path self-clouded, underneath
  The ever-conscious chill of death.

They babble of the fuller life,
  Unswaddled of the mummied clay,
  Whose cerements hide the upper day
That shines serene above the strife
  Of this poor charnel crypt, and cry,
  That they are happiest still, who die.

Who holds it cowardice to shrink
  Before the fearful truth, — That none
  Of all Time's myriads, — never one
Whose feet have crossed the fatal brink,
  Has ever come to breathe our breath
  Again, and tell us what *is* death?

We know that into outmost space,
  Snatched sheer of earth, the spirit goes
  Alone — stark — silent: but who knows
The awful whitherward? — the place
  Which never deepest-piercing eye
  Had glimpse of, into which we die?

Who knows? — God only: On His word
  I wholly rest, I solely lean,
  — The single voice that sounds between
The Eternities! No soul hath heard
  One whisper else, one mystic breath
  That can reveal the *why* of death.

— I think of all who've passed the strife;
  Pale women, who have failed to face
  With bravery of common grace

Their daily apprehensive life,
  Who yet, with straining arms stretcht high
  Through ecstasy, could smile, and die: —

Of little children, who would scare
  To walk beneath the dark alone,
  Unless some hand should hold their own,
Who've met the Terror unaware,
  Nor knew while breathing out their breath,
  The angel whom *they* saw, was Death!

And I am comforted: because
  The love that bore these tremblers through
  Can fold its strength about me too,
And I may find my quailing was,
  As theirs, a phantom that will fly,
  Dawn-smitten, when I come to die.

Therefore I cleave with simple trust,
  Amid my hopes, amid my fears,
  Through the procession of my years,
The years that bear me back to dust, —
  And cry, — "Ah, Christ, if Thou be nigh,
  Strong in Thy strength, I dare to die!"

A BIRD'S MINISTRY.

FROM his home in an Eastern bungalow,
In sight of the everlasting snow
Of the grand Himalayas, row on row,

Thus wrote my friend: —
"I had travelled far
From the Afghan towers of Candahar,
Through the sand-white plains of Sinde-Sagar: —

And once, when the daily march was o'er,
As tired I sat in my tented door,
Hope failed me, as never it failed before.

In swarming city, at wayside fane,
By the Indus' bank, on the scorching plain,
I had taught, — and my teaching all seemed vain.

'No glimmer of light, (I sighed,) appears;
The Moslem's Fate and the Buddhist's fears
Have gloomed their worship this thousand years.

'For Christ and His truth I stand alone
In the midst of millions: A sand-grain blown
Against yon temple of ancient stone,

'As soon may level it!'—Faith forsook
My soul, as I turned on the pile to look:
Then rising, my sadden'd way I took

To its lofty roof, for the cooler air:
I gazed, and marvelled;—how crumbled were.
The walls I had deemed so firm and fair!

For, wedged in a rift of the massive stone,
Most plainly rent by its roots alone,
A beautiful peepul-tree had grown:

Whose gradual stress would still expand
The crevice, and topple upon the sand
The temple, while o'er its wreck should stand

The tree in its living verdure!—Who
Could compass the thought?—The bird that flew
Hitherward, dropping a seed that grew,

Did more to shiver this ancient wall
Than earthquake, — war, — simoon, — or all
The centuries, in their lapse and fall!

Then I knelt by the riven granite there,
And my soul shook off its weight of care,
As my voice rose clear on the tropic air; —

"The living seeds I have dropped remain
In the cleft: Lord, quicken with dew and rain,
Then temple and mosque shall be rent in twain!"

THE BRAHMIN'S TEST.

I.

A Pundit sat with knitted brows,
  His Shaster on his knees,
And in his hand the printed page
  Which men from overseas,
Disciples of the foreign faith,
  Had brought to vex his ease.

II.

"How can I know,"—he questioned sad,
  "If this or that be God?
Since first the Vedas taught the fear
  Of Brahma's frown or nod,
My fathers worshipped him, and I
  But tread the paths they trod.

III.

"This Christ—whence came He? As I read
  Of all He wrought and said,
The teaching of our Holy Books
  Seems childish babble spread

Before my eyes, and doubt's simoon
  Swirls round and round my head.

IV.

"Yet strangely fastens on my heart
  This wondrous story told:
Not thus within *our* sacred scrolls
  The Sages wrote of old:
— O Christ, so near and human-sweet!
  — O Brahm, so far and cold!

V.

"All joy is drained from life; all sleep
  Forsakes these eyes of mine:
No self-negation soothes my soul,
  No pilgrimage, no shrine:
My Vishnu's wisdom shows so weak, —
  This Jesus', so divine!

VI.

"Why should I shrink to end the doubt
  That racks my spirit so?
— Is he Supreme? Then he can shield
  His life against my blow:

I'll test him at the dagger's point
  This very night, — and *know!*"

VII.

— Grim darkness gloomed the Hindoo fane
  As through its silence stole,
With hard-held breath and quivering limbs,
  The Pundit to his goal
Before the idol, where he sank
  With terror-smitten soul.

VIII.

"O, what if *this* be God indeed,
  And when he feels the smart
My dagger deals, he from his throne
  In direst wrath shall start,
And clutch me in his grasp and spill
  The life-blood from my heart!

IX.

"Yet, what if Christ be God indeed,
  His *avatàr*, the peace
That reconciles this warring life,
  And gives, when time shall cease,
From cycles of soul-wanderings,
  At last — at last release!

X.

"O, not to scoff at Brahma's power,
  I come — nor to deny:
And if my wounding proves him God,
  He'll *know* the reason why
I strike ; — and should he slay me, still
  I dare the truth, and die!"

XI.

Full in the idol's breast the blade
  Was plunged : — There came no moan!
The Pundit dropped with stifling joy
  Upon the pavement stone,
Sobbing — "*My Brahma is a lie, —
  The Christ is God alone!*"

THE GRIT OF THE MILLSTONE.

Yea — we give thanks for daily bread,
  With words that breathe a reverent air,
  And marvel much that others dare
Eat of their Father's bounty spread,
  Nor bless Him for His boundless care.

The dainty wheaten loaf, like snow
  Of triple-bolted white, we break,
  And with an inward zest partake,
(We call it gratitude) and know
  'Tis only ours for Jesus' sake.

Yet let a hidden dust of grit
  But set our teeth on edge, and how
  Each turns to each with captious brow,
As (of all thankfulness acquit,)
  It were our right to murmur now.

O, graceless prodigals that we be!
  Self-beggared so, and turned adrift
  To starve, or back to come and lift

Appeals for hireling fare, shall we
  Fret if a sand-grain mar the gift, —

When we should take the menial's place
  And meekly say, whate'er befall:
  "Give as Thou wilt, or large or small,
Since 'tis of Thy so marvellous grace
  That Thou should'st grant Thy gifts at all!"

So, hap what haps, with chastened mind,
  Let us receive the mercies spread
  Around us, all unmerited,
Nor, as we use them, seek to find
  The grit within our daily bread.

TRUST.

A SONNET.

CONSIDER: — Were it filial in a child
 To speak in such wise? — "Father, though I know
 How strong your love is, having proved it so
Since earliest memory; and though you have piled
Store upon store, with care that has beguiled
 You oft of needed ease, thus to bestow
 Comforts upon me when your head lies low, —
Yet in my heart are doubts unreconciled.
 — To-morrow, when I hunger, can I be
 Right sure, for bread you will not give a clod,
Letting me starve what time you hold in fee
 (O'erlooking lesser wants) the acres broad
Won for me through your life-long toil?" . . . Yet *we*,
 In just such fashion, dare to doubt of God!

HARVESTED.

'TWAS late in a life's pale autumn,
  The green of the blades grew sere,
And ripened and rich and mellow,
  The corn was filling the ear.

On the marge of the moistened Springtide
  Had the living seed been sown;
And under the dews of heaven
  In shade and in shine had grown.

The heats of the noon would wither,
  At times, its marrowy leaves;
It bent to the brunt of the tempest
  That darkened the summer eves.

The rasping Nor'east would buffet, —
  The mildew follow the rain;
But all, in the eye of the Master,
  Was helping to fill the grain.

He knew how to temper and portion
  The sunshine, the wind, the air;
He saw what its roots most needed,
  He watched what its blades could bear.

And once and again he lopped it,
  For sake of the fruit, — he said;
And bravely it bore the wounding,
  Though under the hurt, it bled.

And so when the dim November
  Came with its mists at morn,
And the autumn frost into whiteness
  Was bleaching the tasselled corn, —

When the yellowing ears were fruited,
  And the grain was sweet to the core,
The Master who saw that it needed
  To stand in the field no more, —

For the cold and the mould of winter
  To shrivel and shrink the leaf,
Said, — "Put in the sickle, Reaper,
  And garner my full-ripe sheaf!"

BABY-FAITH.

O, BEAUTIFUL faith of childhood! — How
It beamed to-night on the up-turned brow
Of the little kneeler who bent to say
Her prayers, in her innocent, dreamy way.

"And doesn't my darling" — (soft I said,
As I pressed my lips to the flossy head) —
"Long to be good, and by-and-by
Go to a home in the happy sky,
Away and away above yon star,
Where all of the sweet child-angels are?"

She lifted her drowsed and sleep-dewed eyes,
And I saw a ripple of trouble rise
That shimmered across their haze of blue,
And kept the gladness from breaking through.

"I think — I would like to go," — she said,
Yet doubtingly dropped her silken head,

And clasped my hands in her fingers small;
"But then — *I'm afraid that I might fall*
Out at the moon!"
                    Her baby-eye
Saw only an opening in the sky,
A radiant oriel whence the light
Of heaven streamed wide athwart the night;
Where the angels lean, as they come and go,
A-gaze at our world so far below.

She mused a moment in pretty thought;
Then suddenly every feature caught
A glad, rare sparkle, and I could trace
The dawn of the trust that flashed her face:
"But God is good: He will understand
That I am afraid, and He'll take my hand,
And lead me in at the shining door,
And then, I shall be afraid no more!"

THE LITTLE WATCHER.

"So tired looking out of the window,
  And up at the cold gray sky,
And down on the streams of people
  That never and never get by!

"I wonder how long I've waited
  Alone in the darkness here
Watching to see him coming;
  I think it must be a year.

"I needn't have stood and listened
  For his footstep day by day,
If only I'd heard them saying
  A word of his going away.

"For nobody thought to tell me,
  Though I missed and missed him so:
But all of the house seems empty,
  And that is the way I know.

"I'm hungry to have him kiss me,
And I think as each night grows dim,
He will come — if his heart keeps aching
For me, as mine aches for him.

"I've waited so long to tell him
That I've heard two robins sing;
And I want to show him my snowdrops,
And to ask if it's almost Spring.

"Hark! there's a step on the pavement
Like his, — but . . . it passes by:
I'll hide in the shade of the curtain,
Where nobody sees, and cry."

— Ah, pitiful little weeper
Nursing your griefs so dumb,
You are but one of watchers
Whose darlings will never come!

TO THE UTTERMOST.

A SONNET.

OF His high attributes, beyond the most,
  I thank my God for that Omniscient Eye
  Beneath whose blaze no secret thing can lie,
In His infinitude of being, lost.
I bless my God, I am not wrecked and tossed
  Upon a sea of doubt, with power to fly
  And hide, somewhither in immensity,
One single sin, out of His reckoning crossed.
For even there — self-conscious of its thrall,
  Might spring the terror ; — " If He knew the whole,
  And tracked this skulking guilt out to its goal,
He could not pardon ! " — But, or great, or small,
  He knows the inmost foldings of my soul,
And knowing utterly, forgives me all !

NOTES.

1. THIS celebrated portrait of Mona Lisa, the wife of Francesco Giacomo, is considered one of the four finest portraits of the world. Leonardo da Vinci had it on his easel four years, and then reluctantly gave it up, declaring it still unfinished. This great Master is well known to have been one of the most versatile men of his age, being scarcely less remarkable as architect, engineer, scholar, musician, than as poet and painter.

2. Vittoria Colonna, one of the most beautiful and accomplished women of her time, was the early-widowed wife of the Marquis di Pescara. She remained true to the memory of her first love, though sought in marriage by some of the most noted men of Italy. She was forty-seven, and Michael Angelo, sixty years old, when they first met: and there is no foundation for the impression that any emotion beyond that of the purest and most reverent friendship ever existed between them: she was the only woman he ever knew, — the one whom *he* might have loved, if she had never loved and lost.

3. *Sebastiano del Piombo*, (so named because he was invested with certain Papal *Seals*, from which he drew his revenue to the utter neglect of his art,) was a contemporary of Michael Angelo, and for a time his pupil, — having been his assistant while he was painting his frescoes in the Sistine Chapel. He was so given up to indolent self-indulgence, that it was almost impossible to compel him to fulfil his engagements, and finish his pictures.

4. It is scarcely possible that the two foremost artists of the modern world should not have met whilst they were severally executing their great works, — one covering the walls of the Vatican with his immortal creations; the other frescoing the ceiling of the Sistine Chapel. Biographers are fond of imagining a rivalry between these Masters, but close scrutiny reveals none. Raffaelle's admiration of Michael Angelo is well attested, and he was willing to owe something to him, inasmuch as his improvement in *form* was marked, after his study of the frescoes of the latter.

5. According to Vasari, it was Piero de Medici, whom his father, Lorenzo the Magnificent, used to call his "fool son," who put this indignity upon Michael Angelo.

6. In one of the sieges of Florence, the artist Palla, quite celebrated in his day, seized, with the connivance of the Tuscan Government, large numbers of the art treasures of the city, under pretence of a nominal price, and sold them to the King of France, — thus enriching himself through his country's ruin. The Donna Margherita Borgherini, who owned the masterpiece of Jacopo Puntormo (*The History of Joseph*), braved the power of the *Signòri*, and defied them to take her pictures.

7. It was wholly through the loving championship of his pupil, Poussin, that the fine painting of Domenichino, *St. Jerome's Communion*, was finally hung opposite *The Transfiguration* in the Vatican.

8. Albrecht Dürer married, after this, a wife of his father's choosing, but his wedded life is always represented as unhappy.

9. This incident did occur, as his biographers relate, in the boyhood of Murillo.

10. The apology for introducing verses whose interest has passed with the hour for which they were written, is, simply, that they drew from the Princess of Wales an autograph letter to the London editor who first published them.

Cambridge: Press of John Wilson & Son.

www.ingramcontent.com/pod-product-compliance
Lightning Source LLC
LaVergne TN
LVHW050522100826
845148LV00002B/414

* 9 7 8 1 4 2 5 5 2 0 7 0 0 *